Why me?

Seven people living with AIDS

*This book is dedicated to all Buddies
because they have chosen the path of
love by volunteering to do this work.*

Why me?

Seven people living with AIDS
Interviewed by Margje Koster

Floris Books

Translated by Tony Langham and Plym Peters

First published in Dutch under the title
Waarom ik?! Aidspatiënten over zichzelf en hun leven.
by Christofoor Publishers, Zeist 1992
First published in English in 1993 by Floris Books.

British Library CIP Data available

ISBN 0-86315-169-8

Printed in Great Britain
by The Cromwell Press, Wiltshire

Contents

Foreword

by Sheila Cassidy

Once upon a time, a man known as Jesus of Nazareth went to a party — a dinner party with some friends. It wasn't a very formal party, because his friends weren't very formal sort of people, but it was very merry. The people there were enjoying themselves as only the poor can, with a joy and lightheartedness that takes no account of the hardness of life or the uncertainty of the morrow.

Jesus was clearly at home among his friends and I imagine he let his hair down and talked and drank wine and laughed and danced with the merriest of them. It has to be admitted that by some people's standards they were a pretty motley lot: alcoholics, drug addicts, transvestites and gay men and women by the score. Many of them were artists, musicians, writers and TV personalities, men and women whose spirits were too large for their bodies, who lived and loved foolishly, who burned the candle at both ends, all too aware that it would not last the night. Not all were gifted people though, some were what we would think of as the dregs of society, drug pushers, prostitutes, boys who sold their bodies for cash to furtive sad men seeking an illicit comfort that their wives couldn't provide. There were those too who said precious little about themselves, ashamed perhaps of the work of their own hands, the way their lusts drove them when times were bad.

It was a noisy party, with wild music filling the night, and in every corner there were people talking, drinking, or exploring each others faces and bodies with little or no regard for the onlookers. Perhaps it's no wonder then that Jesus' other, more respectable contemporaries were shocked to see him keeping such company.

"I don't know how the Master can bear to sit next to that woman!" said one blue-rinsed matron. "Surely he knows what kind of a woman she is! Good Lord! He might catch something from her, sitting that close ..."

"You're right, Muriel," said her friend, a retired Colonel. "Do you see that young man on his left, the good-looking, rather effeminate one? He was up before me on the bench a couple of days ago, for soliciting, bold as brass, in front of the town hall. A fine was all I could give him. Monstrous. If it was up to me, I'd ..."

Another elderly woman who had kept silent up till now whispered: "You don't suppose the Master could be ... You know, *that* way?"

"Really, Joan! Of course he isn't. After all, he's a rabbi!"

A quiet clergyman standing next to her opened his mouth to say something but, thinking better of it, closed it again and looked distinctly ill at ease.

So engrossed were they in their conversation that they didn't see Jesus approach them until there he was, smiling in their midst.

"Lovely evening," he said, "aren't you coming to the party?"

"What, *this* party?" asked Muriel bluntly.

"Not my sort of people, old man," said the Colonel, "not my type at all. Frankly, I'm not sure you know what you're doing, mixing with that sort."

Suddenly, the Colonel faltered, because Jesus had stiffened and his face was white with anger.

"Don't you know," he said softly, "that I've come to call sinners? *These* are the people my Father loves, these prostitutes and pimps, tax-collectors and junkies. These are His people and these are *my* people. When will you understand that you can't buy your way into the Kingdom with wealth or privilege or your self-righteous good works? When will you learn to take the scriptures seriously? You listen to the readings in Church and you complain about modern translations wrecking the beauty of old texts — but you still haven't a clue what the prophet meant when he said: *What I want is mercy not sacrifice.*

"Will you listen to me for a moment and try to understand. Do not judge these people. It's not your business to judge them. You know nothing about them and yet you condemn them unheard. What do you know about their parents, their childhood, their lives, what struggles they've had, the pain they've endured? Who asked *you* to be judge, social worker, and executioner all in one? Judge not or you may find yourself judged and the result may shake you to your roots. Go back and read Chapter 11 in Wisdom: *In God's sight the whole world is like a grain of dust that tips the scales, like a drop of morning dew falling on the ground. Yet he is merciful to all ... he overlooks men's sins so that they can repent.*

"Don't you understand that God loves everything that exists — how could he not love the work of his own hands? If God did not love these people just as they are, wounded, troubled, confused, he would not have made them the way they are. If he didn't wish them to exist, they would just vanish into thin air. They continue to exist because he holds them in existence with exactly the same love that he holds *you*. You're all his people. These are your brothers, and mine. Could you not try to understand them?"

This book, this beautiful and unique book, is a rare look into the hearts and lives of Jesus' rowdy, wounded friends. They told their stories, and now she tells them to us. They are amazing, humbling stories of the sort of people most of us never meet and are therefore secretly afraid of. Not only do these young men and women speak of how it is for them to have AIDS, to be facing a premature and distressing death but they have very different backgrounds, unique and frequently very troubled. As we listen with Margje, silently, not interrupting, not commenting, not judging, it is impossible not to be moved, for here is a story of grief and disaster. Again and again we hear it: "My parents did not get on, they quarrelled, they drank, they abused me;" "My mother died;" "My father ran away;" "My brother was killed." How, one wonders, did these children survive to reach maturity, let alone the wisdom they now possess? Yet under all the rubble of their broken, apparently wasted young lives, we glimpse the face of God.

Like Jean Vanier, the founder of L'Arche movement for the mentally handicapped, I work with broken people. My work is similar to that of Margje Koster, for my job is to accompany men and women facing death from cancer. They are frightened people, often angry, struggling to make sense of what is happening. Their "why me?" is the cry of those who feel themselves victims, yet know not what they have done. They look in the mirror at their mutilated faces, their wasted bodies and they weep with shame and frustration as their bowels and bladders betray them. It is not difficult to feel an outcast, a leper, when you stink of urine or have only a fetid hole where your nose used to be.

Such people are poor indeed for they have lost not only their health and their independence but their sense of personal worth. They feel themselves useless, a failure, inhabitants of the strange and lonely world of the sick and the disfigured. But the cancer patients, my people, have an easy time compared with those with AIDS, for society does not feel the same about AIDS as it does about malignant disease. Cancer is an OK disease, like high blood pressure or diabetes. True, we're a little embarrassed by people's misfortune and prefer to spend our leisure time with the fit and healthy like ourselves. But AIDS, oh AIDS is very different. *Nice* people don't get AIDS, (though of course even we forget those poor innocent haemophiliacs). But everyone knows that you get AIDS by having the wrong sort of sex: perverted sex, or sex with the wrong sort of people. It's not the sort of thing you'd catch from your wife or your fiancée, you get it from prostitutes, from promiscuous men and women, people who've led dirty lives. The other way you get it is from needles, dirty needles shared at horrible, debauched parties or in dirty squats in decaying houses. AIDS people are simply not respectable ...

Why is it, I wonder, that people get so hot under the collar about AIDS? Of course things are better now, because we've all been educated and we know *intellectually* that anyone can get the disease, but somewhere deep in our guts we are afraid. We're afraid because we don't understand it, because it's a mysterious fatal illness and we're afraid of catching it. And because we're afraid, we would rather not be involved, and we shun people, marginalize and condemn them. PWA's — people with AIDS — or those who are HIV positive are afraid to tell people of their illness because they're afraid of losing their jobs, of being refused life insurance, or hounded out of their homes. They're afraid their children will be victimized at school and their wives or partners shunned.

So people with AIDS have a double cross to bear: they are ill, with no hope of ultimate cure and they live in constant fear of rejection by society. No wonder they need a lot of support. What then can *we* do, to right this terrible wrong, to treat AIDS for what it is, a very serious infectious disease that needs skilled treatment and compassionate care? Once we have understood the *facts* about AIDS, how we can get it and how we can't, then we need to try to understand those men and women whose

life situation makes them vulnerable to this disease. Once
we understand our broken people, then we will cease to
be afraid of them and we will be ready to welcome them
into our hearts and homes as they deserve.

Understanding people is a way of seeing people with
God's eyes, looking with love and compassion into their
turbulent hearts, asking not, "why did you do it?" but
"how can I help you?" We need a sort of infra-red God
detector to seek out the Christ hidden under the rubble
of messed up lives. Once we have learnt to do that, we
are long way towards becoming the kind of loving, non-
judgmental people that Christ calls us to be.

There is another, almost selfish reason, for fitting
ourselves to accompany these people, and that is that we
might share in their very special gifts. God has made a
covenant with his people that, however great the suffering
he calls them to endure, he will be there, with them in the
darkness. It's easy to make a pious statement like this, so
that we can feel all warm inside, without really believing
it. If you read this book however, you will catch a glimpse
of what I mean. I believe that God reveals his love in a
very special way to those who suffer. Sometimes it is a
very obscure "shewing" but it is there if we look for it.
There are two things in particular which happen: one is
that, because people have been so radically stripped of all
that most of us take for granted, they are given a height-
ened appreciation of the ordinary. Listen for a moment to
Paul, one of the people in this book:

> My life has been totally changed with AIDS. It has
> become very rich. I feel as though I've started a
> completely new life ... At last I have a feeling that
> I am alive and I can do and enjoy things which
> are fun. For example, going to the countryside. I
> enjoy this so much now. I never used to notice
> the flowers and the birds singing, but now I go to
> the park to look and listen, and it's wonderful.

This is the testimony of a young man in the last months of his life. He is so ill that he can no longer live alone but has to be cared for in a nursing home. He has had pneumonia five times and he has lost the sight of one eye. "I am afraid of dying," he writes, "very much afraid," and yet he counts himself rich. It's curious isn't it?

The other way in which those in severe adversity catch sight of God is through the tenderness of those who minister to them. There is something both holy and healing about being cared for, being listened to by someone with a loving, non-judgmental heart. For people from poor backgrounds, to experience true tenderness is a miracle indeed. As Sidney Carter writes in his poem about Mother Teresa:

> No revolution will come in time
> to alter this man's life
> except the one surprise
> of being loved.

To provide a "safe" space in which troubled people can be listened to, in which they can speak of what is in their hearts without fear of reproach, judgment or condemnation is to love in its richest meaning. Love is not so much about holding people in an embrace as about "holding" them in one's heart. It is this unconditional loving by professionals, volunteers, friends or family that reveals to people that they are loved and therefore loveable, that they are worth more than many sparrows. "Pain," said philosopher Stifter, "is a holy angel which shows treasure to man which otherwise remains forever hidden." As we read these stories and marvel at the lack of bitterness, the generosity of spirit of those wounded people, we are sharing not just in their pain but in the treasure which is rightly theirs.

Acknowledgments

Seven young people were prepared to share their impressive lives with you. They had the courage to tell me, with absolute candour, what happened to them and how they coped, or are still coping, living face to face with death.

Because of the nature of the conversations and the highly confidential and intimate nature of the information, I have decided to omit the questions I asked and leave them to tell their own stories.

After recording three or sometimes four long conversations, I tried to follow the "thread" of their lives with the written word. Then I gave them the story to read and correct. It was only when they had the feeling that it was their own story, that they were telling it themselves, that they gave permission to publish it. Each one of the conversations was a meaningful encounter which enabled me to write their story "with all my heart and soul." I am very grateful to them all.

The fact that I was able to write this book is also due to the great contribution made by my husband, Leo Koster, not only in typing and correcting the text, but also by being prepared to step aside again and again, allowing me to carry on my work with people suffering from AIDS.

I would also like to express my warm gratitude to Arij van der Vliet. He encouraged me to write this book, and his confidence in me helped me to overcome the obstacles. His advice and his readiness to listen to my experiences have been a tremendous support.

Margje Koster

Why me?

An introduction by Margje Koster

I will not easily forget my first encounter with Monique and her circumstances. I visited her at home, where she was spending a few days. She had to go back to hospital that evening. A few months earlier she had been told that she was HIV positive. Although this did not get through to her at the time because she was suffering from a psychosis, it gradually became real to her and she realized that it amounted to a death sentence. She was seriously ill. At first, her arms and legs had been paralysed, but after a daily programme of excruciating exercises she had learnt to move her arms again with the help of her husband Rob. Rob had not only encouraged her in this, but had also actually done the exercises with her and constantly praised her courage and perseverance. However, she would never use her legs again.

It looked as though she would die within a few months, and as it was her and Rob's wish that she should spend the last period of her life in familiar surroundings, the Metgezel Foundation had been asked to make this possible by providing both practical and emotional support in the form of Buddy help. After the first phone call I visited Monique at home to see what her home situation was like and to judge which Buddies might be able to work there in a fruitful way.

Monique was lying on the sofa in the living room and I was hardly through the door when I was engulfed by a flood of questions alternating with experiences in her life and feelings which had overwhelmed her at that time.

All her inhibitions were removed by her illness: she had
no reservations, and she could and did say anything.
She was beyond shame. Crying, she shouted at me about
the inhuman treatment she had received in the psychiatric institution where she had been sent in the first in-
stance, and her sense of outrage filled the room. In the
middle of a sentence her mood changed completely and
she told me, glowing with love, how much she loved Rob
and everything he did for her. Then despair took hold
again and she screamed: "Why has this happened? Why
me? What did I do wrong, why do I deserve this? Why,
why me?"

Obviously I could not give her an answer to this, and in
fact she was not asking me for one. The only thing I could
offer her at that moment was to suffer with her, touched
by her despair, and be together without saying a word.

I left deeply moved, and for the first few days after the
visit I was struggling once again, following a confrontation
with a patient suffering from AIDS, with questions about
the meaning of life.

Less than a week later, I visited a patient in the hospital
one evening. I took the underground train to Amsterdam
Central Station at about ten o' clock. Because of an
incident in the train, I started talking to the man who was
sitting next to me. We both got out at the central station.
Meanwhile, he had told me that he was a policeman and
was on the way to work. Walking to the exit, he asked me
what sort of work I did. When I told him that I worked for
a Buddy organization he asked me whether I met the
patients themselves. I said that of course I did, and very
briefly described what my work was like.

He was surprised that I wanted to do that sort of work
because he said: "After all, you are working with people
who have become infected through their own fault. They
just live irresponsibly. I don't want to have anything to

do with them. I have young children." Then he walked into the station square. I walked home filled with indignation.

One of the most difficult things for us to deal with is to face our fellow humans without prejudice; with regard to AIDS, this seems to be impossible for many people. Because AIDS can be transmitted through certain kinds of sexual contact or the use of the dirty needles of drug addicts, it immediately conjures up a world of fear and prejudice in many people. This was not the first time when talking about people who were HIV positive that someone had remarked openly that it was their own fault. Again and again I am astonished by the simplistic conclusions which some people draw about the lives of their fellow human beings.

The answer to the question "Why me?" — a question which nearly everyone has to cope with when they hear that they are incurably ill — is crystal clear to these others. The patient is a homosexual, a drug addict, or a prostitute, and so on. He or she may be heterosexual, but in this case they may have been living a promiscuous life — and therefore "it" is their own fault. So that's why!

The idea which they have of these groups of people is not usually based on their own experience, but on what they have heard about them, and it is therefore usually unrealistic. Nevertheless, they have made up their minds and pronounced judgment; in general, they haven't the first idea of the influence of their judgment on the person they are judging.

Unfortunately, I still find that people feel forced to keep silent about their disease to others, because they know that otherwise they will be mercilessly rejected. To go through the process of dying, whispering mysteriously about the cause of the illness until death, is unbelievably painful and makes it virtually impossible for the patient to accept their situation. After all, accepting the end that is coming is closely related to accepting the life which went before. And to do this you need an environment which accepts things with you. You need people who do not judge, who are prepared to look with love at what was good and what was not good for you, together with you. People who have respect for the choices which you sometimes took of your own free will, but also often by force of circumstance, and who are prepared to suspend their own judgment.

It is only when another person is allowed to be who he or she was, that there is room to become more the person that he or she really is. An interest in, and respect for the path this person has chosen and may still follow, is absolutely essential. To do this, you need courage. Courage to constantly modify your judgments. Courage to learn to cope with the resistance which you feel when you notice that you are different from another person, and which leads to judgments. The courage to ask yourself why you should reject a homosexual so mercilessly. Is it possible, for example, that confusion about your own sexuality could be the reason why you cannot accept the sexual nature of another person? Are you really free in your judgments, or are your judgments like a "life buoy" giving you a sense of support and security?

I am convinced that knowing yourself is an important precondition for being open to other people. All the reasons for judgment or prejudice disappear when you can sincerely and honestly dare to look at your own one-sided shortcomings and small mindedness. This can lead to an interest in the path which another person is following, or has taken. I am also convinced that your judgment is less severe and your understanding greater, if you are able to see the whole context in which the life of the other person has taken place.

I am always deeply affected by the stories which AIDS sufferers tell me about their lives. The road behind them was often one of denial and rejection, and in many cases they experience this again because of their illness.

Just imagine what it's like to learn to cope with such a terrible disease and to constantly come across people who are afraid of you because of it. I often feel indignant when I hear the prejudiced comments about people suffering from AIDS because the judgments are usually based on generalizations, or what is externally apparent.

There is no such thing as the typical AIDS patient. They are all individual people, each with his or her own very personal life story. In many cases they have a very emotional life behind them, and now have to come to terms with it because they are face to face with death. The answer (if there were an answer) to the question: "Why me?" — a question which many people ask themselves at a stage of fury and disbelief about the fate that has befallen them, is reserved for people who are going through this process. It is shameful that there are people who consider that they have the right and the insight to know the answer.

Although the doctors gave Monique another three to six months to live, she lived for almost two years after my first visit. The burning question was with her until the end, but the sound and colour of the question constantly changed.

The first few months after she had become aware of her situation, the question was loaded with anger and disbelief. It was a raging against life: her life, her fate. She screamed with anger against God, or anybody else who came near her. Often these were her husband, family or friends, but when she went to the doctor she also sometimes asked people who happened to be in the waiting room: "Why me?"

During the course of her disease I increasingly had the feeling that the strength with which she initially displaced this question outside herself, was used to an ever greater extent for looking inside herself. I was there only once when she put the question directly to herself and she was able to formulate what this terrible disease had brought to her: "I have become more mature, more loving. I intensely enjoy silence and the small things which used to pass me by." And then she was even able to ask: "Is that why?"

These were valuable moments when she came closest to acceptance, though her question had not been answered.

As soon as she became aware again that her illness would end in death and that she would have to let Rob go, despair returned and she railed against life again.

At the end of her life she was able to accept that the question would remain unanswered while she was still on earth. However, she was convinced that she would be given an answer after death: "I will knock and the door will open, and then I will know at last."

Joeri (35)

I was born in Amsterdam, the second son of parents who didn't get on at all. My brother was four years older than me and always bossed me about. I never got on well with him at all. What I remember about my early childhood is that my parents still lived together and that it was therefore a good time for me. Not because it was much fun, but because my father still lived at home. I was crazy about my father, and when he left us, I missed him terribly. That is why my early childhood was the best time of my life. Apart from that, I remember that in those years my mother often used to make small pancakes which I ate in the street with my friends.

My life was lived out in the street, even when I was very little. At home there were always problems between my parents. They often quarrelled terribly, and I made sure that I was out of the way.

I never really had a home; I was a child of the street, with no God and no discipline. No one had any control over me. I lived my own life with my friends, and usually this meant getting up to all sorts of mischief. Occasionally I would accept what my father told me, but when things came to a head I still went my own way. My father had a guest-house and if things were bad at home, he would go and we wouldn't see him for days on end.

Eventually my mother found out that he had another woman. Then they divorced after terrific arguments. I was about eight years old and I hated my father going. I often visited him in his guest-house, but in a way I became even more indifferent about all sorts of things.

I didn't go to school much. I wasn't cut out for sitting at a desk and doing what the teacher said. I was usually at the cattle market because I was crazy about animals, particularly horses. When my father still lived at home I used to go on and on at him because I wanted a horse. He didn't think a horse in the attic was a very good idea, and later on I could understand what he meant.

My friends and I spent most of our time playing dangerous games. Of course this was very exciting but it also led to some very serious accidents, particularly in my case. I really believe that I was born unlucky, because I had one accident after another.

The first major accident happened when I was seven years old. We were playing on a building site. The workmen were having their lunch and had left a large boiling pot of tar unattended. The pot glowed red. I started stirring it with a stick and wanted to throw the tar around but I couldn't. Large drops of liquid tar landed on my face burning big holes in my skin. It only just missed my eyes but I needed plastic surgery and it took six operations to make me look better. I still have large scars on my face.

We were also regularly in trouble with the police. Sometimes I ended up at the police station for stealing, sometimes for vandalism. We were notorious.

When I was ten I had another serious accident. We often climbed about demolition sites. Often the floors had been taken out of buildings while the walls and roof were still standing. In many cases there was still an attic where former inhabitants had left all sorts of things. Sometimes we would find an old war trophy.

We had climbed up a drainpipe to the attic of one of these derelict buildings, when the attic caved in. I fell 24 metres with my head hitting joists with nails at the level of every floor. My friends thought I was dead, and they ran to my mother shouting: "Joeri is dead, Joeri is dead." Of course, my mother panicked. When she found me she thought I really was dead. I looked terrible; my whole head was black with bruises. In hospital they put me in intensive care and my mother was sent home with the news that I had a multiple fracture of the skull and wouldn't make it. But clearly I was very tough.

When I came out of hospital, my life in the street started all over again. Mostly we stole mopeds, rebuilt them for motocross and went racing in isolated fields or simply through the neighbourhood. The police were always chasing us and sometimes they closed off the area so that I couldn't escape. Then they'd take me with them.

Meanwhile, my mother had gone off with a Turk. Later on, she married him. She didn't want to look after us. She'd told the police that they'd better put us in a home. I thought this was really rotten of her and shortly after she went, this is what happened. At first, my brother went to live with my father, who had also remarried, and I went to my grandmother. She was a lovely woman. When my parents quarrelled at home, I usually went crying to her. She would console me. Granny did everything for me but she had no control over me either. I ate, drank and slept at her house but for the rest I lived on the streets. It still bothers me, the way my mother abandoned us then. I haven't really forgiven her yet.

People from child welfare used to be after me because I hardly ever went to school; the education inspector tells them about that sort of thing. After the fifth year in primary school, I didn't go to school at all and I didn't have any secondary education. My father gave me a bicycle for my eleventh birthday. Of course, I took off straightaway. At one point a tram frightened me, and because I was startled, I hit the wing mirror of a lorry and then landed underneath the cab. Again the police went to the house, while the family nervously came to the hospital where I had been admitted yet again in a critical condition with a fractured skull. And as though this wasn't enough, I was run over again by the same tram — line 10 — in the same place — nine months later. I simply ran into the tram while I was playing. And ... believe it or not, I had another fractured skull. I think I simply had no sense of danger, because after all that time in the hospital I simply went back to my old life, looking for excitement and adventure with my friends.

Meanwhile, we used to go to a youth club where there were lots of other young people also looking for adventure. There was a man there who was actually a criminal. We often had to do dangerous jobs for him. He was dealing drugs, and this always led to problems, for example, from people who owed him money. One group would be given the task of visiting people like this and torturing them. I joined in with this. We did the most cruel things for him. He called himself "the Boss" and we called ourselves "the Gang."

When we did a job for him, he'd pay us. We were really in awe of him, and there was no question of refusing to do something he ordered; you simply did what you were told.

In the end, the police picked me up and put me in an institution. I lost my freedom, and that was very difficult for me. Of course, the most difficult thing was to obey the rules, because there was a strict regime. I got on quite well with the other boys who were there.

Then I was transferred to a youth detention centre in another place. This was also a closed institution, but not as strict as the first one. They said they were going to keep me under observation. But as soon as I had the chance, I decided I would escape. Generally I behaved quite well. Just as long as they loosened up a little and then, when I had the chance, I would get out. Whatever I was doing, I was always planning or looking for ways to get out. Then I would hitch-hike straight to the youth club until the police picked me up again. Occasionally, I would be let out for a holiday, and then I didn't always return.

I was transferred again, this time to a prison which had various sections on the site. At first, I was placed in a reasonably open section. This meant that I was allowed to work on the land. I liked that; when I was a child I really wanted to be a farmer because I liked animals and nature so much. But still, I regularly ran away from there as well, and then I was transferred to the closed section. There was no more question of working on the land; I was put in a cell — luckily not with bars, but with reinforced glass. We had to do various jobs, but most of the time you simply sat in your cell. Even so, I still succeeded in escaping a few times, and in the end they simply didn't know what to do with me. I could not be educated, and my guardian from the child welfare department came to tell me I could go home because I was considered a lost cause. Obviously I thought this was great, because I'd been locked up for two years.

When I went home to my granny, I was fourteen years old. Then I went out to sea on a boat for almost two years with Smit Tak. It was heavy, rough work, and I liked that. I left just before my sixteenth birthday. I had had enough and once I was back home, before I knew it, I was joining in the life of crime with the gang. I started using drugs. At first, the Boss gave me the drugs free, but as soon as I could no longer do without, I had to pay a lot of money for them, and that meant robbery, breaking and entering and so on.

My father gave me a moped for my sixteenth birthday. One evening I went out on the town with my friend Micha, and I had an accident. I drove into a post and my friend smashed right into it. He died straightaway. I had a shattered leg and a broken hip. It was all very terrible, especially for his family. I would rather have lost my leg. I could have accepted that better than his death. He was my best friend.

I was bedridden for six months and then I needed a period of convalescence, but they didn't allow me to stay for that because once I was walking about again, I became involved in a fight. I was on drugs and kicked a man so hard in the face that he nearly died. He ended up in intensive care and I was back in the police cell. The police said that if he died, I'd be sentenced for murder. In the end, it was attempted murder, because he lived.

I was sentenced to six months in prison. This time I didn't go to a youth detention centre; I was sixteen and still came under juvenile law, but the judge said I was no longer a child. So I went to prison, where there were only adult criminals. Actually I had quite a nice time there; it wasn't too bad. The other prisoners were quite nice to a youngster like me.

As soon as I left prison I went back to the youth club. Where else could I go? At my granny's I was bored out of my mind. I was a freeloader and actually heavily addicted to drugs like most of the members of the gang. The gang now consisted of sixty people. We were some of the heaviest criminals around. We were a sort of mafia. Breaking and entering, assaults, torturing, shooting — we did everything for the Boss. Always under the influence of drugs.

I hadn't been out of prison for very long when I shot at a policeman during a raid at the youth club. Fortunately I didn't hit him, but anyway, shooting at a policeman is taken quite seriously. Once again I went back to prison for four months. The gang kept in contact with me. We were brothers and sisters to each other and didn't let each other down when someone was inside.

My brother was also locked up in an institution and then went to prison a number of times. He was on probation and was committed in custody, but fortunately this didn't happen to me. When that happens you lose your freedom for good. They can bring you in for a minor offence because the parole officers keep a careful eye on you. My brother had also belonged to the gang all that time; he was a master thief and was really good at breaking into places and stealing things. They called him the "gentleman gangster" because he was always very well dressed. He was completely different from me; I was always scruffy. We didn't get on at all. He always tried to boss me about and if I didn't do what he said, he just kicked me in the face.

Meanwhile, my mother had divorced her second husband who was an alcoholic and used to beat her. After the divorce, he still would not leave her alone. Then my brother and I did him over. My brother hung him up from a rope on the stairs until he was unconscious. Then he untied him and beat him up. So that was the end of him. Even though my mother had abandoned us, she was still our mother and we wouldn't let anyone hurt her. During that time I went back to live with her for a few years. Meanwhile, my granny had gone into an old people's home and she died shortly afterwards.

My mother had quite a difficult time with me. I was still hooked on drugs and even stole from her when I had no money to buy any. At that time I did many drawings and paintings under the influence of amphetamines and heroin. Usually these were religious paintings, for example of Jesus on the Cross. I don't know exactly how I came to do these. I had been to a Christian school where we always started with prayers and my granny had been a very religious person. Perhaps this influenced me. It's possible. But I was also inspired by the drugs and I didn't only do religious paintings but also many faces. The eyes of those faces were very real and frightening. They just followed me through the whole house, and in the end my mother stopped letting me hang them up. It was as though they radiated a negative strength. My mother threw them away because they frightened her. Now that I'm clean, I can't draw or paint any more.

Because we were on drugs in the gang, we were no longer in contact with our feelings. We were completely merciless, but we didn't realize it. We were actually dependent on the Boss. In fact, he drew us all into the underworld, and once you were in the gang, you couldn't simply leave it. It even happened that if one of us stepped out of line, he would come with a syringe. A few big rough guys would take hold of you and pump you full of drugs so that you couldn't move for a while. Anyone who betrayed the gang, or tried to get away, would get an unexpected visit from some of the members and there wouldn't be much left of him. So you wouldn't think about going away. Apart from that, I was really in awe of the Boss. He was a sort of father figure for us all. Now I know better.

When I was twenty, I met a woman and fell in love with her. She was more than twenty years older than me and came to the youth club because I had nicked a sound system from her son. Her son was afraid of me, so she'd decided to come and tell me that I'd better give the sound system back. I thought that was great. I invited her for a meal and that's how it started. Shortly afterwards she went on holiday to Italy and I simply followed her, trusting to luck, because I had no address and only knew the name of the place. When I arrived, I found her sitting in a cafe. It was fate.

I went to live with her and tried to kick the habit for her sake. I was given methadone, and things went well for quite a while. I still managed to give her quite a few problems though. I drank rather a lot, and whenever I met anyone from the gang I was lost. Before I knew it, I was injecting again, making great problems for my girl-friend. Sometimes I wouldn't go home for weeks at a stretch and threw her money around. She had quite a bit of money from the sale of a guest-house where she had rented rooms to prostitutes. I managed to get through most of it; I was good at spending money.

Whenever I used drugs and saw how sad it made my girlfriend, I hated myself. I had no strength of will at all. I was crazy about her and wanted to do everything for her, but again the drugs were stronger and got the better of me.

This self-hatred caused me to overdose six times. Each time I ended up in intensive care, and they managed to keep me alive. Obviously this was also hell for my girl-friend. But I really believed she was better off without me. One night I walked down the motorway into the traffic. I wanted the cars to smash me up because of the way I was treating her, but although it was dark, every car missed me. It was as though I had a guardian angel, and it just wasn't to be. After doing something like that, I resolved to improve my life, but before I knew where I was, it started all over again.

Fortunately my girlfriend and I also had a lot of fun together in between times. We often went on holiday. I would drive her car because she couldn't drive. I didn't have a driving licence but I was an excellent driver and I never caused an accident.

Once they asked me for my driving licence at the border. We put on such a wonderful act together that they believed us. We said that we had left our papers in our hotel and asked the border guards if we could go and make a phone call. They said that was alright and of course we drove off when they weren't looking.

When we went abroad, we stayed in three-star hotels. We'd take an extra case, toothbrush and pyjamas, and when the holiday was over, we'd leave it behind in our room so that they thought we'd gone out for the day. By the time they'd realized that we'd done a bunk, we were back home. Of course, we always left false names.

Sometimes I worked. For example, I worked in the port loading and unloading bales of rags, and for demolition firms. I liked that. I always did heavy physical work and this suited me.

In October 1990 I heard that I was HIV positive. I had been suffering from strange complaints for quite a while, particularly walking. I often fell down in the street, and in the end I could hardly stand or walk. My GP admitted me into hospital where they did a lumbar puncture. Probably they also did a blood test. In any case, the doctor came to ask me whether I wanted to know the result. He said he could only help me if I said yes. Otherwise I would have to go home and he wouldn't be able to do anything.

Well of course I wanted to know. He said: "You're HIV positive," as though I'd know what that meant; I'd never heard of it. I asked him what it was and he explained that I had caught the AIDS virus and that there were no medicines to treat it. It was my death sentence. It was a terrible shock; I simply didn't want to know. I cried a lot and was terribly afraid. I thought it was so unfair. I kept thinking: why me? I've already had so much misery in my life. Now that I'd finally kicked drugs through my own willpower, this had to happen.

Apparently I had a fungal infection in my brain, for which they gave me medicines, as well as a non-malignant tumour. There was nothing they could do about that. It had affected the central nervous system in my back, which made walking so difficult.

I was allowed to go home with the medicines and immediately took the train to see my girlfriend, who was in a women's prison at the time. The doctor had told me that there was a big chance that she was also infected. I went by train though I had great difficulty standing and walking, and then I told her. At first she didn't know what HIV positive meant either, but it soon became clear to her when I explained. She had a test which proved that she was also infected. That's the worst thing of all for me and makes me feel so guilty. I was infected by a dirty needle and the drugs only made our life miserable. To cap it all, I infected her.

As she was HIV positive, she was dismissed from her job shortly afterwards. For the first year after the diagnosis she was very angry with me. I found this very difficult to live with, though it was understandable; she'd already suffered so much because of the drugs and had always tried to get me off them. Moreover, two of her children were also HIV positive because they used drugs. And as if that wasn't bad enough, she was also going to die herself from AIDS.

At first, I couldn't bear that thought. I was so angry with myself that I slashed my face and cut my wrists. But then later on, I thought it was cowardly to get out and leave her all alone.

After leaving hospital, I went to live with my mother. Luckily she said that was alright, for where else could I go? My girlfriend couldn't look after me any more. Soon I couldn't walk at all, and was in a wheelchair. This was really terrible for my mother because my brother was infected as well as me, and he also started suffering from all sorts of symptoms of the disease. So she had to look after two ill children, as well as my brother's drugs problem, because he was still injecting and needed money for drugs. For her, it was total hell.

Luckily I had been clean for quite a while before I became ill. I had managed to do this with the help of my girl-friend.

At first I was really afraid of death. Actually, it was above all a fear of the unknown. It worried me all day long. I cried a lot in the beginning. Now this has changed because several people have appeared to me in my room. Of course this sounds mad, but I'm not crazy, it really happens.

First, there was a man with neat, long white hair, bare feet and loving eyes. When I was about sixteen, I met him once together with my friend on the Keizersgracht. We were out stealing when he spoke to me. He had a ruck-sack on his back and loose fitting trousers and was also barefoot. He asked us for something to eat but I didn't have anything. I gave him some money and showed him the baker's. Suddenly he disappeared, just dissolved into thin air. Later my friend said it might have been Jesus, but who knows? In any case, this man suddenly appeared by my bed a few months ago. He was wearing a white robe. He didn't speak a word but merely shook his head. I think that he meant that my time had not yet come. At first I thought it was someone from the hospital, but when I looked closely I saw his bare feet and recognized him. He only came once. But my father and my grand-mother regularly visit me. My grandmother died when I was twenty and my father when I was twenty-six. I can talk to them just like that. My father is waiting for me and says that many of my friends who have died are also there.

Because of these encounters I am no longer afraid of death. I have also asked God for forgiveness and he has given me this. What still keeps me here is my girlfriend. Apart from that, I no longer want to live. I really long for my father, and though it may sound mad, I'm really quite happy now. Happier than before my illness. I know that

I will go back to heaven and will soon be with my father. Then thankfully, this difficult lonely life will be finally over. Peace at last.

I was diagnosed as having AIDS two months ago. I had double pneumonia, and even suffered a cardiac arrest. They resuscitated me so I am still here. Meanwhile, my brother has also been infected with AIDS and is blind in one eye.

I have started to accept my illness a bit more but I will never be able to accept the fact that I infected my girl-friend. This is really terrible for me. I now live independently in a special house. My girlfriend looks after me most of the time, together with the home help and my Buddies. Luckily we are good friends again; we love each other dearly, and actually the illness has brought us closer together. She is also suffering the first symptoms of AIDS: pain and tiredness. This is very difficult.

My brother still lives with my mother. It will be very difficult for her when neither of us is here any more.

When I was a member of the gang hooked on drugs, my conscience didn't trouble me. The drugs totally wiped out my conscience. When I look back now I really regret many things. I made a terrible mess of it, a total waste. I think that's awful. How in God's name can I put things right?

There's only one ray of light. I don't know where it's come from but I'm convinced that I can have another go here on earth and that I can put right everything I did wrong. I will be back, I'm sure of it, and this gives me a sense of relief. I've learnt some hard lessons in this life. I will never touch drugs or drink again. Never! I hope that in my next life I'll be able to put things right for the people I've treated so badly in this life. Of course, it will all be very different then, but perhaps I could be a sort of social worker, so that I could do something positive for them and pay my debts. I would also like to work to combat the drugs trade. In the end, it's drugs which ruin many lives, as they have mine. If I'd been able to avoid drugs, things would have been very different for me and my girlfriend.

May 1992

On November 19, 1992, four months after his brother, Joeri died. The last months of his life were very problematic. Although he was bed-ridden he could be incredibly aggressive and threatening to his friends and those looking after him. His contact with his old "friends" continued as before. He sold them sleeping tablets which he got on prescription from his doctor and a specialist.

When he was quite haggard and too weak to struggle, an incredible tenderness and love came to the fore in him. The last four weeks of his life were filled with an unbelievable peace and love, and he showed those around him much gratitude.

Joeri died with a radiant smile on his face, with the conviction that his father was waiting for him.

November 1992

Merel (31)

I was the youngest in a family of eight children, and the brother who was just above me played an important role in my early years, as my protector. I was in his group of friends and so I played mainly with boys. But I do remember a few girlfriends. I was a very vulnerable, open and sensitive child and I had a sunny character. Three major disasters managed to overshadow this sunny side for many years.

The first disastrous incident in my carefree life was a serious accident involving a friend. We were standing by the roadside, hand in hand, ready to cross over. I told him we couldn't cross yet, but he ran across anyway, and was run over by a tram right in front of me.

I immediately ran home and my mother later told me that she found me, white as a sheet, on the step of the kitchen door, unable to utter a word. My friend had been crushed by the tram so badly that they needed a crane to lift it off him. He lived, and after years of rehabilitation, has turned out reasonably well. For me this was the first conscious experience of danger in the world. What intrigues me is that he told me, much later, that while he was lying under the tram I sat by him on my knees giving him words of courage and consolation, while I am sure that I was in shock at home, unable to speak for a long time.

The second traumatic event was when our family moved to another part of the country in connection with my father's work. My father was a minister, and his vocation had a particular influence on me and on our whole family.

I was nine years old when this enormous change took

place. I never felt at home in the place where we moved. We lived on a busy crossroads opposite a bus station where the buses were always waiting with their engines running. They vibrated so much that I could feel it in my very bones. And I really hated the wind which was always whistling over the flat landscape, so that I constantly felt uncomfortable. These external circumstances had a great influence on me. I missed the peace of our previous house and really suffered from the change. I was very nervous, always had a tummy-ache and couldn't eat a bite of food before going to school.

School was an even worse disaster. I was horribly teased for all sorts of things. A minister's daughter is always a good target for bullies, but they also teased me about my appearance, because I wore glasses and wasn't allowed to do certain things at home. I was very sensitive, while my classmates were more aware, more socially adept and insolent, as well as meaner. I missed the protection of my brother, who'd moved to another school, and felt deeply unhappy. It was the end of my carefree childhood.

The third incident was when I was ten years old and my father had a heart attack. It happened at my oldest brother's wedding, where I was a bridesmaid. The mood was very joyful and I felt beautiful in my bridesmaid's dress and very proud of the role I had been given. During the reception the mood changed from one extreme to the other. I was called by my brothers and taken to a room where my other brothers and sisters were waiting. You could have cut the atmosphere with a knife. One of my sisters was crying and said my father mustn't die.

My father's condition was so serious that we had to take turns to say goodbye because everyone expected he would die. When it was my turn, I was called into a small room where my mother was, and where my father was lying on a mattress on the floor. I could see that he was in great pain and felt helpless and confused seeing him like that. All this happened in just a few minutes while we were waiting for the ambulance; it was unreal and at the same time very intense.

My father was put in intensive care, and because for a long time my mother had to travel up and down to the hospital to be with him, the household was run by my older brothers and sisters. I couldn't cope at all with the chaos this caused. My father survived, and came home after a while, but in a sense he was handicapped. Obviously this was very difficult for him, and he became very tense. After some time he tried to go back to work, but it was all very difficult.

Our whole domestic routine had changed because he was at home so much, and this constantly led to stressful situations. Suddenly we had a father who was interfering with the day-to-day running of the house, though he'd been home very little before his illness. Obviously this was difficult for him, as well as for us. It constantly led to quarrels and I couldn't cope with it at all. In addition, I became aware, during that period, of the values and norms which applied in our family, and of the interrelationships. The way in which my parents dealt with my brothers' and sisters' interests was in total conflict with my sense of justice. There was something in me that strongly protested against the fact that personal interests were subordinate to "what the outside world thought." It didn't seem loving to me when my sister's boyfriend was thrown out because she had to finish school first. This was really very sad for my sister. And there were so many quarrels about all sorts of things. We couldn't do this and we couldn't do that. It was so difficult.

As a minister's family, we lived in a sort of glass cage, which was very difficult for my parents. The effect on me was that I started to withdraw into myself. The situation at school, where I was still being bullied, only aggravated the feeling. I started to live a life of my own which no one could control. I pinched money from my mother's purse and shared out the sweets in the schoolyard. I started telling lies to everyone, and even when I was caught out, I would deny everything. No one understood what was the matter with me and I didn't say anything. I was completely locked inside myself and wouldn't let anyone in.

That was the start of a long and very lonely road. Obviously my parents were deeply concerned about the problems I was causing. For example, they had me psychologically tested. One day my mother asked whether I would like to go to another school, and I seized the opportunity with both hands. So I did the sixth year at another school where the atmosphere was a lot better. It didn't have a great influence on my reclusiveness, though my mother often made attempts to break through to me. At home, there was still a lot of tension and there was no change in my suspicion about the rest of the world.

My father was no longer able to work, and on the doctor's advice we moved house so he wouldn't constantly be confronted with his work. We moved house in the summer holidays, at the end of my sixth year in primary school.

For the first few years at secondary school I was still bullied a lot and not accepted by my schoolmates. But I lived my own life and went my own way. At home, I was an easy child, fitting in with the family, but in fact, I lived my own life alongside them. Of course, this was all done secretly, which meant I constantly felt under pressure. I always made secret arrangements with boys and often wasn't where I said I was. I always ran the risk of being caught out and had to be careful about everything I said. I had shut myself off to the values and norms which applied in our family so that I was unable to see the good things that were there as well. I was very lonely, though I spoke my mind when I was with boys, but of course I couldn't find what I wanted with them either. This was sex, which was an exciting adventure, but didn't answer my deeper needs. The only person with whom I really shared anything was a girlfriend. She has remained a great support to me to this very day.

You could say that from the age of eleven, I was looking for values and norms with which I could identify, but how do you find them? I discovered them with great pain and difficulty, through experience. I moved from one relationship to the next. Without really making any choices myself, I let myself be carried along by anything I came across. This meant excitement and adventure, but also a rift with my parents and my brothers and sisters with whom I no longer shared anything. In addition, my conscience was troubled by all the lies I told, so that my self-esteem certainly wasn't very strong.

My relationship with my father was a big problem. On the one hand, I quietly resented him because I had the feeling I always had to move aside for him. We always had to be quiet because he couldn't take any noise; we forever had to consider him because he was weak. This was a terrible pressure which oppressed me a lot. I was an adolescent and being "quiet" was very difficult. On the other hand, I longed for his attention; I wanted something from him that he probably couldn't give. I suspect that the experience of suddenly having to say goodbye to him when I was ten years old also influenced my relationship with him afterwards, although I still can't describe exactly how. I was looking for father figures very early on.

I first had a relationship with an older man when I was fifteen years old. I had known him a while and he was always very nice to me. At first he was someone I could confide in; someone who listened to me, took me seriously and accepted me. Later, there was also some physical contact, but we didn't do more than cuddle each other. I broke off the relationship when I found a boyfriend of my own age who also came to my home.

After secondary school my parents suggested that I should go to England as an "au pair" for a year. I had broken up with my boyfriend. I had just scraped through my examinations to my great surprise, and I had no idea what I wanted to do next. Everything was arranged within a week and I left, attracted to freedom. It was a relief to leave my double life at home behind me. After some problems in the first family, I managed to find a place in another family. In this foreign country I again found security with an older man, and started a relationship with him.

When I went back to Holland, I took up nursing. I did an advanced training course where a great deal of time was devoted in the first few years to the student's development, both at the personal and social level. In this respect, I learnt a lot during my training. The feeling between the students was open and friendly. There was a warm atmosphere, and the fact that people would simply hold each other when something was difficult, or sometimes when something nice had happened, was a relief. I wasn't used to this sort of thing. At home we had always been rather distant with each other, both physically and emotionally, and this was an environment where I felt comfortable. Not that it was always very easy. I had to confront my own contradictory feelings and found it difficult to accept. I was looking for the real me and the essential aspect of other people, and this is where I took the first steps.

Meanwhile, I had formed a relationship with a divorced man. It was a very complicated situation between us because he drank a great deal and had problems following his divorce, and I couldn't cope with that at all. But one day he talked to my father and told him how we were living. This was a big shock for my father. My parents had suspected that we were living as man and wife, and when we broke it off shortly afterwards and I had yet another

boyfriend, they found it completely impossible to understand.

We talked and they asked for an explanation, but I was
unable to explain; I could only cry. I didn't want to disappoint them, but the rift between their world and mine
was now so great that it was too much to ask them to
understand my way of life. I think I was still too young to
have any understanding of their way of life. Moreover,
everything that happened was still happening to me from
outside and I was still largely in the dark about why I was
doing what I was doing. But I did know that I no longer
wanted to be responsible to them.

All in all, I felt so confused that I decided to break off
all contact with them. I told them that I wasn't angry with
them, but wanted to go my own way. In that year I sort of
bade farewell to my youth. Initially this was accompanied
by negative feelings. I felt the pain of everything I had ever
lacked and I explained it away to myself, telling myself
that was how it had been and I would have to get on with
it. It was only a year later when I found I had some good
memories of my childhood, that I contacted my parents
and went to visit. I never really confronted them. I don't
think I dared take the risk of losing them altogether; after
all, I loved them a great deal and never wanted to hurt
them. But that year I did let go of the expectation that
they would understand and accept me, and decided to
follow my own feelings and be responsible only to myself.

Leaving the Church was a struggle in itself. In an
attempt to hold on to something familiar, I was still going
to Confession, but afterwards I stopped going, so I could
freely interpret my faith later in a new way.

When I had passed my diploma I was twenty-three
years old. I didn't start working straightaway, but travelled with a girlfriend. I went down the coast to Portugal,
and then went on alone. I think I became infected with
the HIV virus during that period. On the trip I came into

contact with someone, who, I think in retrospect, was probably a drug addict. In addition, I had some symptoms of tonsillitis and a fever, which usually happens after you become infected. I'm not completely sure, but almost.

Three months later, I was back home. I wasn't pregnant and I though I'd come out of it alright, and that life would just go on. I picked up a relationship with a former boyfriend (an older man), and during the time I was with him I think I gradually became aware. Because of everything that happened to him, I started to understand that everyone can't be a friend in life, and that people sometimes destroy each other. I soon began to realize that not everyone can be trusted or wants love.

Up to then I had a very naive idea about people. If I liked someone, I soon opened up to them. But for the first time I was thinking to myself: "Merel, just watch who you are getting involved with." I think I started to grow up a little.

I only really started to be careful when I became involved with Johan, my next boyfriend, who is still a friend now. I got my driving licence and started to work. I also started relating to my parents again, on my own terms. I began to realize the importance of getting on with them and wanted to fight for our relationship. But the most important step for me was the decision to be honest from then on. Before that, I had shut myself off from the world and had told lies to conceal what I was really doing. It had become second nature for me. I was so insecure that I always wanted to be more beautiful, bigger and better than I really was. I couldn't value myself, and created a world in which I could manage to accept myself.

Johan was my great example. He's twenty-one years older than me and had been suffering from manic depression for a few years when I met him. He had been institutionalized several times, and this also happened during our relationship. One thing was very important to him: he

wanted to be honest in his life, honest to himself and to
the rest of the world. It was only through him that I really
became aware how broken I was inside, and this was a
very painful realization. But it meant I could also finally
listen to my own deep longing to live in harmony with
myself and the rest of the world. This had really been the
reason why I had shut myself off from the world. At home,
I had had the feeling it was impossible, but this had been
completely snowed under by the illusory world which I
had created. Obviously things didn't get better overnight.
It was quite a fight for me and my partner to succeed, but
when I became aware of these things I couldn't go back
and didn't want to. I was all too aware how many people
I had hurt by avoiding any confrontation with myself. I
would always give up on a relationship when it got too
close to me, leaving the other person confused and wondering what had happened. I had made a firm decision
that I wanted to be the person I was. I would let myself be
that person. In the end it didn't matter what other people
thought about me and I was prepared to take responsibil-
ity for my own acts.

The people around me didn't really understand my
relationship with Johan. They saw only his manic depression, but I could see more. I saw his perseverance, sincerity and a great sensitivity and respect for life. With
him, I came across real life. This was often terribly difficult, but we had made a real choice for each other and
wanted to share our life. This is what we both wanted.

In 1986, I started to develop all sorts of complaints;
skin problems, candida (a vaginal fungus), tiredness,
swollen glands, etc. It was one thing after another. I kept
going back to my GP with complaints, but I don't think he
took much notice. After a while I had a feeling that all
these things were related but I wasn't quite sure how.
I started to play volleyball, because I thought it might
be that I wasn't very fit. I visited a homeopath and an

46

iriscopist and started going to yoga lessons, but nothing
really happened. Meanwhile, my work was very demand-
ing, and so were Johan's constant bouts of manic depression. Coping with all this required tremendous energy and
of course I couldn't always manage. Sometimes I could
help to drag him through or prevent him from having to
go back into hospital, but I no longer had the energy to
make the effort and this led to constant problems between
us. It wasn't that we didn't love each other — that wasn't
the problem. But there came a point when I could no
longer cope with my work as well as being a support and
refuge for Johan. My priorities were too often with Johan.
He usually came first, I was less important, and this
simply couldn't go on.

In retrospect, I think the process of dying had already
slowly started, though I didn't know it yet. I no longer had
any energy left for people and things outside myself.
Actually, I didn't really even have enough for myself.

In fact, everyone had doubts about our relationship
and they didn't bother to conceal them. My family,
friends, and even the doctor, said it was understandable
that my health was suffering. They said it wasn't possible
to live with a man like Johan. Gradually I started to
believe them. I thought the way I felt was due to stress,
because I couldn't cope. And of course, living with Johan
was no fun. First, I decided to go on holiday on my own
and that was quite difficult because Johan was dependent
on me in a way, but I simply had to go — I just couldn't
go on.

Then I decided to go and live on my own. It was all very
sad for both of us, but I couldn't see any other way.

It was August 1990, and everything was packed when
I became really ill. I'd become as thin as a rake, only
weighed forty-eight kilos and could hardly breathe sometimes because I felt so constricted. The doctor sent me
to hospital for some tests and I asked him to do an HIV

test myself. In 1986, Johan and I had talked about it. At that time, AIDS had been in the news a lot, because it was a new thing and of course I knew that I had been at risk. But as we had had a sexual relationship for a few years, I thought that if I were HIV positive I would have infected him already so there was no point knowing. He didn't really agree, but left me free to decide. Afterwards I simply didn't think about it and repressed it up to that time.

Anyway, a few days later I was called to see the doctor in the ward. I was very ill and was taken in a wheelchair to a room where they told me I had pneumonia and that the HIV test was positive, so I had AIDS. What happened next is very difficult to describe. I thought: Oh God, I've got AIDS, and realized immediately that this was my death sentence. But instead of being terribly shocked, I had the feeling that something opened up inside me. For a moment, I felt whole; as though I was no longer being broken.

Before being diagnosed as having AIDS I had always been looking for the source within myself. I thought there must be a spring of love, call it God or whatever, but I could never really make contact with it. With my head I knew it was there. I read about it, but I couldn't feel it. And then, at the point that the doctor told me, it was as though it was suddenly put in my life. Something exploded inside me and I had the clear feeling there was something which said to me "And now I am here for you." Then I suddenly felt convinced that I was right after all about there being a God. All my channels opened up and I knew where my source was.

It all sounds rather deeply religious, but this is really what happened. It was actually a very positive experience, even though I certainly realized that I would die, and that from that moment nothing would be ordinary any more. No more dancing or cycling or running, for example, and very little spiritual energy. I had already lost so much concentration. Later I cried a lot about this in bed.

For the first few weeks I felt as naked as a baby. I had the feeling that everyone must understand now, what sort of life I had lived, and strangely that was quite nice — there was a sort of wordless openness. The people who came to visit me also seemed naked to me because the insecurity they felt as a result of the fact that they knew I would die, was quite tangible. We simply couldn't hide anything from each other and I thought that that was how people should always be with each another, absolutely open. It's less lonely than always keeping things from each other.

The first person I told was my girlfriend. That was the evening of the day I found out. We discussed how we would tell my parents and Johan. I decided to go to my parents myself the following evening, to tell them at home. Although I had a fever and was very weak, I thought that was best, so that's what I did. My girlfriend and my sister came to pick me up and I'd warned my parents and told them I had bad news. Johan was there as well when I told them, and because of my warning they were expecting something very serious. My father said they had thought it might be cancer or AIDS.

Of course, my parents were very sad, but they said, "We accept this as the way it is. You're our daughter. We love you and we're here for you." It was all very moving. My mother gave me her gold bracelet, I was to have inherited it after her death. I was very moved by that.

For Johan it was very difficult. In my parents' house we couldn't be close. For that reason there was unfortunately a distance between us, but I think that there was also an understanding between us, now that we knew the reason for my inability to support him, as though we realized why I had had to leave and that it was not because we didn't love each other. It all became clear.

Of course, the news that Johan was also infected was very difficult. Shortly after my diagnosis he had a test which showed that he was positive too. This was a very bitter pill for me to swallow, and for him as well, of course. It's something that keeps bothering you even when you know that you didn't know at the time, etc. After all ... I infected him. That's something I can't get round. Fortunately it hasn't moved us apart but has actually brought us closer together.

Although it didn't look as if I would survive the pneumonia, I did survive. It's already eighteen months ago. When I was discharged from hospital I went to live on my own, as we had planned. It didn't seem a good idea to change our minds. I wouldn't have the strength to support Johan any more, and I'd have to look after myself (and so would he). We see each other regularly, because he is and always will be the most important person in my life.

Up to now I haven't really had any rebellious feelings. There have been moments but that's all. Before I became ill, I was convinced that everything that happens to you in life, is meant for you and has a purpose for your development. Up to then, that had been my experience and I never had the feeling anything serious could happen to me. So I never had the feeling: Why me? Why me, and not someone else? I accepted that this was the path I had to take straightaway. My path. And that I would also be given the strength to follow it. It reminded me of a feeling that I had before I became ill.

I felt there were all sorts of qualities and strengths in me which were simply lying fallow. I couldn't use them because I had never had to do anything difficult. I often had the feeling something would happen or something was waiting for me which would require all my qualities and strengths; and now this has happened.

It has become my task, my purpose, to die, and that's

the greatest thing which can be required of you when you are so young. It is also a challenge for me to do this as positively as possible, not only for myself but also because I would like to do something for other people. I don't know yet what, but I feel a strong need to do this. At first, this led to some ambivalence in my feelings.

At home I often felt that I couldn't join in because everyone thought I was too young. It was as though there was a message that I had nothing to say anyway. Now I have the feeling that perhaps I could help others, for example, by talking openly and honestly about my own death. So this means that now I am old enough.

For the people around me it's sometimes difficult that I am so positive about everything. They constantly want to show me the difficult and heavy side of my illness. I think they are projecting their own importance onto me. It must be difficult for me or nothing makes sense. It's all part of being ill and certainly part of dying. But that's not what it's like for me. Obviously there are days or hours which are very difficult, but usually I'm optimistic and able to see the positive things which my illness has also brought me. I'm developing at a tremendous rate. I feel as though I am in contact again with what I was like as a child. I feel liberated, I can be myself again. The sun has risen inside me.

The feeling that everything was happening to me, that I was being pushed from one thing to another without really being involved, has gone at last. I'm holding the reins myself, I can stay with myself and I'm able to persevere much better. My illness is a challenge and I want to get all I can from it every day.

I can move a step forward, and if I don't, that's just a waste. I see more and get enormous pleasure from nature and people. My world has become very small because of a lack of energy but that's actually quite pleasant. I don't think we were really made to become involved with the whole world through radio and television. That's a pressure and makes you weaker. My illness has allowed me to become involved in my own world; to relate to it intimately. I no longer live alongside it, I live in it.

At the same time, I am finishing things off. For me, finishing off means above all doing things differently from the way I did them in the past. Getting right the things I did wrong, as though I am making corrections. Being sorry about what I've done doesn't seem appropriate. There's pain because of the way some things have gone, but no regret. I can say to myself: "That was as far as I'd got as a person and that's why I couldn't do it differently. If I had been able to, I would have."

I have quite good contact with my parents now. I've learned to respect their norms and values. I can understand them better and see that they also have a life behind them in which they were formed by the values of time and their own upbringing. I no longer feel the need to change that in them. And yet the strange thing is that I have once again taken up some of their norms and values. There's quite a lot in some of those things.

There are still feelings which we can't share at all. And we still have different views on certain things. That's why I wasn't able and didn't want to tell them about some of the things that have happened in my life. That's a great pity, but after all the most important thing is that we love each other a great deal, and I can feel their support which is very good.

As my father is still ill and has been preparing for death for several years, there is a special understanding between us. We are in the same boat and sometimes we can share that.

I am trying to prepare myself for death by experiencing the process of dying which started a long time ago. Every day I die a little, you don't just die on your deathbed. Apart from birth, death is possibly the most essential thing which happens in life. I want to be involved in this process. I want to be strong when death comes and let him in like an expected guest, ready for it. I am still searching for what that really means, being "ready for it." Perhaps it means creating peace in myself in which we no longer have to hide anything from one another, in which everything and everyone can be what they are. A peace in which love can flow freely.

I'm not afraid of death, but I am afraid of pain. When I have a lot of pain, or lose my balance, the ground disappears beneath me. I lose my optimism and my confidence. I feel so shut off from everything in myself and outside myself that I become depressed. And it's so terrible to feel that I'm not afraid of death itself. Once someone died in my arms and that was not something to be afraid of. In a way it was a beautiful experience. The way in which the life left the body was very impressive, almost graceful. I looked at it and assimilated it. I think it has helped me not to be afraid, although I never felt any fear of death before that either.

I am convinced that my life is protected by Christ. This is a very strong feeling in me, but I have no image of what it looks like. I have read about it but that doesn't really give me any picture of it either. And I don't really need that. I would like that miracle to remain a miracle. It's beyond our imagination anyway. The certainty that life does not end is a sort of consolation and makes me feel peaceful. I hope I leave something behind me on earth. I like feeling that part of me has helped with another life. No matter how small — a thought or a conversation or something someone touched in me, which helped him. If that's the case, my life has had some meaning.

May 1992

Monique (28)

I was the oldest child in a family of three children; there were a brother and a sister after me. When I look back at my childhood, it's difficult to think of anything good. From the age of four it was all terrible. My parents had big problems and quarrelled a lot. My father drank, was schizophrenic and suffered from religious delusions. When he drank he became very aggressive, it was awful ... Often I had to listen to him rambling on for hours on end about his faith — even if I was dog-tired he wouldn't let me go to sleep. The pressure he put on me was terrible. I was always afraid of him, and his illness made a deep impression on all of us. At school I had a good time, but I always went home afraid and there was no security at home at all.

Because of his schizophrenia he was often compelled to do strange things. For example, he thought that he was being followed by the CIA. He wouldn't allow me to be seen in the street with him because the CIA were not allowed to know that I was his daughter. So I had to walk a few feet behind him. For a small child this was very confusing and frightening.

When I was twelve years old, my parents officially divorced, but my father still came home regularly, and there were still quarrels. There came a point, when I was fourteen, that we could no longer bear it and we went to live in a refuge. They tried to help us function as a family, but this failed because my father wouldn't co-operate. Altogether, we were in that home for a year, but afterwards we were even further apart than before. When we went back home, my father had destroyed the house — at least that's how we saw it. My father called himself an artist and described what he had done as "art."

At that time he often looked at me in a very particular way. It was as though he was undressing me with his eyes. He looked at me in places where fathers should not look. This affected me very much and made me afraid, which meant that when I reached adulthood I had great sexual problems.

The only fun I had at that time was going out with my girlfriend. I have good memories of this. They were the only happy times.

When I was twenty-three, I left home. I had a boyfriend and I went to live with him. He was a drug addict and injected hard drugs. I knew this, but I thought I'd give him a chance, and perhaps he would stop. I loved him very much, and that's why I took a lot from him. I had absolutely no self-esteem and was looking for love. From him I hoped to get everything I had lacked at home.

There were times when he was so wonderful to me that I forgot everything he did to me, but usually he treated me like a rag. He hurt me to the very depths of my soul and I cannot make anyone feel what that is like. I did everything I could, but despite that, he hit me. Once I found another woman's earrings in my bed. He made some excuses, but it was deeply humiliating. In fact my relationship with him was a love-hate relationship, just like the one I have with my father. I just had too little confidence and self-esteem at that time — I'd never accept anything like that now.

He constantly threatened that he would leave, and then he'd come off the drugs and I'd start hoping again, but he always went back to the drugs. He stole and robbed the neighbours, and became involved in fights and so on, and so on ...

The fact that I took so much from him was related to

my situation at home before that time. He was my first boyfriend; I wanted to give him a chance, and I wanted to look after him and be good to him. We lived together for three years and I was always faithful to him but in the end I couldn't bear it any longer, and I left. I didn't know that he was HIV positive, infected by a dirty needle. That only became clear later. Meanwhile I'd met Rob, who was my boss. I worked in his coffee shop and we were in love. We hadn't become involved with each other yet, but because he was there I had the strength to leave my boyfriend. A few years later that boyfriend died. According to his mother, this was from a perforated ulcer. I had serious doubts about that, especially when it turned out that I was infected. The mother has always refused to warn the girlfriends he had after me about the fact that he was HIV positive. This means there is a big chance that they are in turn infecting other people.

I started living with Rob and it was wonderful. His home was peaceful, and for the first time in my life I felt at peace. With him I felt safe.

After a few years I got shingles and became very tired. In the end I could no longer work because I was so tired, and I spent the whole day lying on the sofa until Rob came home. Then I would quickly tidy everything up and pretend I had had a good day. I didn't want Rob to know, and I was ashamed of my tiredness.

In the end I collapsed; I suffered from psychosis and did all sorts of crazy things like lying naked in the garden and phoning America because I thought it was Paradise. The telephone bill was astronomical. I also heard voices in my head, saw the Devil everywhere and told people in the street that a new world was coming. Finally, Rob succeeded in having me admitted to a psychiatric institution. When they asked if I wanted to go — they have to ask when you're admitted — I would say no, and they would have to leave me at home. But in the end that became impossible, and Rob forced the doctor to admit me.

Meanwhile, I'd found out that my previous boyfriend had been HIV positive and Rob wanted me to be tested to see if I had been infected as well. But because of my condition nothing had come of this. Shortly after being admitted to the institution I became paralysed, and even after it was clear that I was infected with the HIV virus, they still insisted that it was psychological and that I had to walk. They put me against the wall, let me go and then told me to walk. I would fall down and was black and blue all over.

I was also locked up in solitary confinement, naked, because they said I was a danger to myself. After a lot of trouble and discussion, Rob managed to have me transferred from that hell to the psychiatric ward of the AMC hospital. There, they knew about AIDS, and I was given proper treatment. I became completely paralysed, but because Rob gave me strength and did exercises with me every day, I managed in the end to stand with some help. I was able to use my arms and hands, but I never learnt to walk again. I have been in the wheelchair ever since.

For the first few months the knowledge that I was HIV positive didn't get through to me at all. I was suffering from psychosis when they told me. I was completely apathetic and couldn't laugh or cry. They might just as well have told a lamp-post. This was very difficult for Rob because he had to cope with it all on his own. When it started to get through to me months later, I cried and screamed for weeks and I was very rebellious. The doctors gave me only three months to live, but that was more than a year and a half ago. Rob motivated me to such an extent that I am still here, and, strange though it may sound, I eventually got used to the idea.

I talked to people about my illness a lot and became very sure of myself. The days that I looked at the floor instead of at people were past. I said everything I thought and no longer asked myself what other people would think about this. I became self-confident and tried to console the people who were sad about my illness. I spent a lot of time thinking about God and felt how much he loved me.

During this period I started living life much more intensely. When I looked in my garden and saw a bird, I felt happy. I learnt to enjoy nature, the sun, the grass, the green leaves, the buds on the green trees and silence — the silence is so beautiful! Many people don't even know silence, they don't take the time for it. These are all things which used to pass me by and now I enjoy them very deeply.

The love around me is very great. My brother, who kept away at first because he couldn't cope with it, has been living with us for quite a while. He and Rob are ready to look after me day and night. This means that we have become very close. I have more friends than I ever had. I feel an oasis of love around me — so many friends who want to do something for me, so many people who are there to help me. And the love which Rob gives me is indescribable! I still enjoy the intensity of life and I still feel the love around me, but I feel much more rebellious. I was diagnosed as having AIDS a few months ago. Death is coming closer and I am angry about the fact that I will have to let go of the love which I have finally found. Gradually I have discovered the happiness that I was looking for, and now I have to die. Why is this? That's what I ask myself all the time. Why me? I was always faithful, I have been a good person. Why not Saddam Hussein? He's a devil, it would be fairer if he had AIDS.

In the evenings I talk to God a lot, and this is a great support to me, but I am still afraid of death. I don't know what to expect on the other side; sometimes I think there will be light and love but at other times I am afraid there is only a black hole.

I am dependent on everyone, which is terribly difficult. Having to ask for everything you want or need some-times gives you a feeling of impotence. There are so many things I have had to give up because of this ill-ness. For example, I shall never have children. The realization of this hurts me physically and something inside me screams: Why not? What have I done to deserve this? I don't understand it. God is love but why does he allow it? I've lost so many things. My work, walking, my energy, taking part in social life, but also so many other little things.

I used to be very quiet and shy, afraid of people and afraid to go out into the street. I shut myself off in my house and hadn't found myself. When I became ill, this changed very rapidly. The confrontation with death meant that at last I could be myself. I have become more self-aware and am no longer afraid of anything except death itself.

My mother has also noticed this. She told me that I'd changed a lot and was much more open. It made me cry so much, and I told her I had always been like that inside, but it had been imprisoned in me. I felt like a flower which had started to blossom, but the bud had always been there inside me.

This was a revelation for me. I enjoy things which I never enjoy before, and time has become valuable. I am very conscious of what I am doing, I have woken up, I am more mature. I am much more involved with other people and I understand what is happening in other people. Life now largely consists of the small things which other people do not notice or do not find important.

When I fell ill, I became a believer; I had been looking for a long time but had been unable to find it. Now my belief is a great support to me. It does mean that I have a different idea of death, as I hope that Jesus will welcome me when I am dead. I feel an empathy with Him because he also suffered so much. When I pray, I have the feeling that He is with me and I feel His support.

Nevertheless, I'm still afraid of death. When a car drives at you, you jump away automatically, it's a natural instinct of survival, and in the same way I keep feeling that I want to jump out of the way of death. I'm still trying to avoid it. And after all, is it surprising? I'm only twenty-eight years old. Twenty-eight, that's not the right age to die. I've only just started to live, to discover what real life is. I cannot accept that it is as it is. But I think that when I die I will have reached the point where I will be able to surrender. That will be my time, and therefore I will be ready for it. Now I am trying to be as positive as possible every day, and that's not easy. I lie in bed virtually all day, my legs are paralysed, I hardly have the strength to hold my own cup when I'm drinking, and talking is becoming more and more difficult. I almost went blind because of a virus in my eye. I can no longer do anything independently, I am completely dependent on others.

In these circumstances, a positive attitude doesn't simply fall from the sky. What helps me is Rob's love and his humour — sometimes we have such a laugh together! My life's dream was always to find a man who would love and respect me, and I have achieved this for he couldn't be more loving!

I have a good relationship with my mother. She has become rather hard on herself and on others, but I can understand that, because she's had a difficult life. It hurts me a lot to know that my death will bring her even more sorrow.

I have forgiven my father. I only talk to him on the

telephone. Because of the circumstances, it's not possible
for us to meet. I think that my death is easier for him to
accept than for my mother. He is a religious person and
keeps saying to me: "You are closer to God than we are."
That supports me.

I am busy arranging my funeral on paper and telling
people my wishes, for example, by choosing music. That's
very difficult because there is so much beautiful music.
The other day Rob said that if they played everything that
I had chosen, they would have to sit in the funeral par-
lour for three days. It made me laugh, I can just see it.

I would like a purple coffin, with a beautiful lining. I
would also like to be laid out at home with many flowers
and my toy rabbit in the coffin, because it was always a
source of comfort to me.

Rob can make a speech and I hope that he says that he
misses me because that will mean that he loved me. Also
that I was always open to people, because I think that's a
very important quality, particularly when you're ill. Many
people around me who also have AIDS are only concerned
with themselves, so they have little understanding for
other people. I would like to urge them all to love each
other and listen to each other because that's what life is
all about.

I don't understand my fate. I keep looking to understand why this happened, but I can't find the answer. I'll
only find the answer when I'm dead. I'll knock and they'll
open up for me and then I can ask: "Why? What is it that
makes me deserve this?" and then I will finally know.

April 1992

*Because Monique had to cope with the fact her illness
meant that she would never have children, she was very
happy when her friend Carla became pregnant. From the*

beginning, Carla involved her closely with her baby's development, and soon Monique was talking about "our" child. She was sure that she would love to be there when the child was born. When the little girl was stillborn at seven months, it was not only Carla who mourned; Monique was desolate. In her sorrow, she promised Carla that she would soon go and take care of her baby.

Apart from Rob's birthday, two weeks later, there was no reason for Monique to go on living. On Rob's birthday she told the doctor she didn't want to go on. She was very ill and had a very high fever. It was arranged with the doctor that on Wednesday (this was on Monday) she would get help if she were still there.

In order to discuss her worries about the possibility of euthanasia, a priest was called to put her mind at rest, and then she asked to be christened. This is what happened. Monique was christened in Rob's arms and then received the last rites. Monique was radiant with joy. All those who were present were moved. Then she became calm and was able to surrender completely. During the following night her mind was clear and she was calm. She communicated intensely with her mother and with Rob. In the morning at a quarter past nine, it became clear that the moment of departure was at hand.

Rob was with her and he told us: "Suddenly the birds in the garden began to sing. I looked at Monique and said: 'Can you hear them?' Monique nodded: 'They are calling you,' I said. 'I think that it's time to go, my little angel. We've had a good time together but now we have to say goodbye. Go on, don't worry about me, everything will be alright.' She looked at me once more and then breathed her last breath. Then at the same moment the candle next to Monique which had been lit by the priest when she was christened, went out. This happened on May 12 at twenty-three minutes past nine.

"I looked into her eyes, and as long as I live I will remember what I saw there at the moment of death. I saw that Monique could see something which she had never seen before. She saw something entirely new, and this made her eyes shine in an indescribable way. I have never believed that there was anything after death, but through her I caught a glimpse of the world on the other side and I am one hundred per cent sure that she's happy there."

According to her wishes, Monique was laid out at home in her purple coffin. We watched over her for three days and nights. The atmosphere around her was light and peaceful. It was a privilege to all of us to experience this. Of course, there was also a great deal of sadness but the main feeling was one of peace and gratitude.

For Rob, this is the start of a difficult time. It will be unbelievably difficult for him, missing Monique. She was a special person with an incredibly positive strength, a fighter who lived life to the full, right down to her toes. She was someone who showed her sorrow unashamedly, but also shared her intense joy unashamedly.

Rob: "I can go on living with what she gave me. The way in which she coped with her illness gave so much to me, and I feel a profound happiness as well as great sorrow, and this happiness shines in me like a bright light."

May 1992

Reinder (33)

I was the second son of a family of shopkeepers. There were two sisters after me. My childhood was very happy and free; we were allowed to do lots of things. My parents had a shop where my mother also worked. As a result, we grew up fairly independently. We could do lots of things, but there was some discipline, and despite our freedom, it was clear what we were allowed and what we were not allowed to do. I trusted my parents; they were there for me when I needed them, but we didn't normally talk about what was happening inside us.

Above all, I remember the wonderful active summers. During my childhood I played a lot of sports. My parents both played a number of sports, and it was taken for granted that we would take them up as well. Everyone was keen on one or more sports and our family won lots of medals. However, it wasn't winning that was really important; we weren't really competitive, the important thing was the sport itself. In contrast, school was terrible — the complete opposite. I couldn't keep up at school. Transferring from nursery school to primary school was very difficult. In the first and second year I often went home with stomach ache, and I regularly wet my pants. Later on, the teacher made a fool of me in front of the class several times because I couldn't understand the lesson.

I was a sensitive child, an outsider, even with other children. I was a dreamer, I preferred playing with girls, I didn't like aggression, and was too soft for the world of the other little boys. I couldn't fight, it just wasn't in my nature and that is probably why I became a target of the bullies and in fights. They would wait for me after school, drag me into the cellar and beat me up. I never told anyone, and kept it to myself, but as a result of all this bullying and the tension which it caused, I had to repeat the fourth year. I was really very miserable.

Later on, at secondary school, life wasn't much fun either. Although I was accepted by my classmates, I had an inner feeling that I was different. I didn't know exactly why, but when the teacher talked about homosexuality during social study lessons I had to summon up all my strength not to blush. "Don't blush, don't blush," I'd tell myself. "I'm not like that, it's not about me, I don't have to be ashamed." This was terrible, these unexpected moments when the thought that I was homosexual threatened to break through into my consciousness. It made me feel utterly unhappy.

When I had to stand in front of the class, I would shake all over and break out into such a cold sweat that my shirt was wet through. I think this was all related to my experiences at primary school.

I was sexually mature at a very early age and played sex games with a friend when I was quite young. When I was fifteen, I came across a book in which I read something about homosexuality. It would pass if you concentrated on girls, though for a few people it would not go away. I broke off with the friend I played the games with, turned to girls, and repressed the idea that perhaps I might be homosexual. For me, this moment was a turning point in my life. Before that time I was still a child playing, but from then on life became very difficult and full of worries. I was often awake for nights on end about something I'd said to somebody. I was afraid of hurting other people and I didn't want to hurt anyone, so this worried me a great deal. I felt very lonely.

Two years later, I found a girlfriend and we had a relationship. This was really a good time. She taught me to talk, which we had never done much at home. Despite the fact that we got on very well together, she felt that there was something not quite right between us. I also felt this, but I really didn't know what it was. I think I'd made a very thorough job of repressing my homosexuality, knowing that I wouldn't be able to talk to my parents about this.

However, I was determined that when I'd finished school I'd go abroad, on my own, to look for somewhere where I could be myself. This helped me to keep going. During this period from eighteen to twenty-one, I was terribly tense. Four or five times a week I had awful headaches, and I eventually failed my exams.

I broke off my relationship with my girlfriend and left for Switzerland to work as a salesman in a department store, in search of myself. The first six months were a lot of fun. We had gone there in a group and had lots of good times together. After six months I met a man who was very nice to me. The next day he forced me to have sex with him.

Something strange happened to me then. I was suddenly in a dark tunnel, and only regained consciousness when it was all behind me. This event and the power which the man had over me — even long after I was back in Holland — had a great influence on my life. Although I repressed the incident, it confused me very much, and I felt lonely and depressed.

After Switzerland, I started to work in America. In the evenings I did a course to become a dance teacher. I didn't want to spend the rest of my life as a salesman. It was only then that it became clear to me how I was. I could think about myself without being afraid of failing to live up to the expectations of those around me. For example, parents don't expect to have a homosexual child,

and because you are dependent on your parents' acceptance and love when you're a child, and you don't wish to
disappoint them, it's very difficult to come to terms with
the fact that you're different.

In America, I still thought for a time that I was bi-
sexual, but there came a point when I knew I was homosexual. This gave me a feeling of liberation. At last, I no
longer had to repress a part of me, and that gave me a
certain sense of peace. I loved living and working there,
and simply didn't think about the fact that I could only
stay temporarily. I was in America for sixteen months.
When I realized that I would have to go home because my
residence permit was limited, I married a girlfriend for the
right of residence. However, the immigration department
found out and I had to leave the country anyway. We only
divorced much later when I was back in Holland.

I dreaded going back again because I had told my
parents on the telephone that I was homosexual and this
had shocked and confused them. In the course of time my
parents did accept it, or at least they accepted it as a fact,
but they didn't talk about it.

I intended to go back to America as a dance teacher. I
saved as much as I could because I was living with my
parents again and didn't have to pay rent. For three years
I prepared for my departure. I had acquired a work permit
and a residence permit and was only waiting for proof
from my employer so that I would be admitted, but this
didn't arrive. Therefore, I had to stay in Holland and my
hopes for the future vanished and I had to start planning
again.

When I was about sixteen, I came across a book about
self-hypnosis. I read that you could use this method to
stop worrying and I was very interested in it. I practised
every day to keep myself under control. I did manage to
suppress parts of myself in this way, but it also gave me

the strength to endure the things that had to be endured. For example, I practised being positive and learnt breathing techniques, and I still benefit from those. Whatever I did, I started the day thinking forward in the morning so that the day was easier to bear and passed more quickly.

One of the ideas in that book was: you have a half-full bottle, so is it also half empty. The question is: what do you look at? I decided to look at the half-full bottle, that is, the positive side; and I still do that now: I look at what I have and not at what I don't have. Because I've done this for years, day in and day out, I have really benefited from it. Adopting a positive approach has become second nature.

I have known that I am HIV positive since February 1990. I had a lot of skin complaints for a few years which just wouldn't go away, but at that time I didn't connect it with AIDS. I sometimes knew about it subconsciously, but never really took it seriously. In those years I was in search of myself. The terrible trembling which I suffered from when attention was focused on me, or when I played the piano when there was anyone there, gave rise to questions and encouraged me to seek help.

I had psychotherapy and a number of things became clear to me. For example, I realized that I was focused too much on the people around me, and didn't stand up for myself. At home, we had always learned to think about other people first and about ourselves second. Therefore I was not very good at standing up for myself. Because of this, I have always been used by people. Everything was always alright — whatever anyone asked me, I always said yes. I couldn't say no, I really had to learn to say no, and to draw boundaries, because it was good for me.

It was a period of self-examination. I had the feeling that whatever it took, it was a matter of my development and I wanted to know who I was. I tried several sorts of therapy and took from it what was important for me. However, I was still nervous. It was less obtrusive, but still a nuisance.

I went to regression therapy and started reading books about paranormal phenomena, life after death, meditation and so on. I was very interested in these things. I'd rather lost track during those years I was unemployed, wondering what the purpose of life was and what it was all for. Reading these books gave me the idea that life is more than visible reality and that all development is important because life does not end with death. This gave me strength and sustained me. My life became richer. I devoured these books and meditated a lot. I was so fascinated by these things that I almost turned my back on the world and locked myself in the house. After a while I realized that meditation is good but that you also have to go on living life. I had gone too far and was in danger of losing sight of reality. When I became aware of this I started turning outwards again.

In retrospect, I see this period as an unconscious preparation for what was ahead. I had a very strong feeling that something was going to happen. I even mentioned this to my therapist. I said to her: "Please help me, something is going to happen. I don't know what, but I want to be ready for it." But how can you prepare yourself for something when you don't know when it will happen? I didn't have the faintest inkling and thought more in terms of work than illness.

Waiting for what was going to happen took too long for me.

I started working in the catering business. It was November 1989. I was soon suffering from exhaustion because it was a busy time in that industry. As I was going to the doctor's very frequently, I mentioned my tiredness. In January he asked me whether I had ever thought about HIV infection. As I was taking a shower

that evening, I suddenly saw it all clearly before me.
Although he hadn't mentioned a test yet, I knew that this
was what I had been expecting and what I wanted to prepare myself for. The strange thing was, it was a great
relief. So this was it. I simply had to laugh. It was only
later, when I talked about it to a girlfriend, that I felt any
emotion. After all, it was not something to be laughed off,
and the time ahead was a difficult challenge for me.

For a while I hoped that I was wrong, but I discussed
the possibility of being infected with my therapist and
then weighed up the pros and cons of a test, preparing
myself for a result that showed that I was HIV positive. I
did this so well that when I heard that I was actually
infected, I was able to accept the fact very quickly.

It's interesting that just before this happened, an em-
ployment agency had sent me to work in a crematorium
to serve coffee; and subconsciously I was attracted to this
job, I had the feeling that I had to go there. It's strange,
isn't it? I went on working there, but when young people
died, I couldn't serve coffee. It made me cry terribly because it was too close to home. I have the feeling that I
went to work because it was a sort of unconscious search
for what "death" really is.

Shortly afterwards — it must have been in about April —
I read an advertisement asking for Buddies. Again, I had
the feeling that I should do something about it. I went
along and, in retrospect, this turned out to be a sort of
therapy.

I only had one girlfriend who knew I was HIV positive.
I hadn't told anyone else. When I told the Buddy group at
a meeting one evening, that was the first real conscious
recognition of the fact that I was HIV positive. I realized
that I would have to work out this situation and that I
would have to share it with others, because I couldn't
cope with it alone.

This encouraged me to become active. Through the HIV café, I found fellow-sufferers, I joined a self-help group, and so on. I realized that there was so much going on inside me, that I would have to deal with that first before I became a Buddy myself. Despite this, I was allowed to join the training course for Buddies. An exercise we did showed me that I was looking for love and support, and this affected me so deeply that I felt I had collapsed and cried terribly. I realized that this is what I had been looking for all those years.

Someone from the group took me home. He wanted to stay, but I sent him away. I regretted that later, because when he left something broke inside me. It was as though I was blown out of myself, I could no longer think, even my thoughts blew away and I had the greatest trouble finally reaching for the telephone and calling a girlfriend for help. It was as though I was completely out of control and I started hallucinating. Luckily the friend soon came and she stayed with me, taking turns with others, for two weeks. I could no longer be on my own and was full of fear because my whole house was full of animals. Monsters constantly came up to me, crawling right up me and when I tried to explain to anyone what I saw, they became even more clearly visible. Whole carpets full of animals walked through my house. It was horrible. Some of them were larger than me. When I started to realize that they couldn't hurt me, I started to get used to them and ignored them. I simply pushed my way through all these teeming creatures and shoved them aside.

Later, when I started to feel stronger than them, I made friends with them so that the fear left me and they disappeared. The emotions which I felt in those weeks were so deep that after this period I didn't dare to cry when I was alone, afraid of plummeting into the depths again.

During this time an agreement I had made with myself

was of great help to me. This was that I wanted to know everything. No matter how difficult, I would face up to it and I would not go mad. I talked out loud to myself and told myself not to panic, reassuring myself that I would not go crazy. I talked myself into staying calm. I tried to do what was good for me, held onto myself, walked round and round the house so I wouldn't stop moving, played music and so on. I wanted to stand up to it and stay in control, and I kept to my own agreement, as this was very important to me. I appealed to my deepest will because I didn't want to go crazy.

There was a lot of aggression in me which I had repressed, but I stayed in control. I discovered that it helped me to do something. I listened to a lot of music, or played the piano. This helped me to stay in myself and I still use this approach very consciously. When anything gets too much for me or when I am afraid, I consciously decide to do something.

Fortunately, this didn't take very long, and after a few weeks I was able to stay on my own again and was in control of myself.

Then I once again went in search of what was happening to me with guidance, and this automatically became clear. The experience with the man in Switzerland came back to me. This was very strong. I relived every experience, and it is only then that I understood that I had had the dark tunnel experience because the shock had driven me from my body. My reaction of shutting myself off when somebody liked me, for fear of being used, also started to make sense. Ten years ago, this experience had influenced my life. Now I was able to assimilate it, let it go and finish with it.

In addition, I discovered that I had never really had a will to live. I existed and that is why I was alive, but I didn't really want to. You might say that I became aware of this because I was HIV positive, and then I was able to make a deep, conscious choice to live. My will to live was born. I wanted to live; I wanted more life and I wanted to be conscious of it. I think it is a shame that it will be short. There are things that I would like to learn, such as drawing, and I have made a start on it. I would also like to do more about music.

Meanwhile, my family also know that I am HIV positive. It was very difficult to tell my parents about it. I understood that they would find it very difficult, and I didn't want to hurt them. My mother's able to cope with it better than my father. She reads about it and we have more contact than in the past. My father is very reserved. Still, there are small things which show me that he's working on it. For them it is a difficult process to learn to accept that they will lose a child. In fact, I have the closest contact with my youngest sister.

Once again I have the feeling that something else will happen. I am not sure what, but there is something I have to do, I haven't finished yet. I think it will simply become clear what it is. Perhaps it's the actual illness that is waiting. I only have twelve T4* cells left. At the moment my resistance is zero. Suddenly I could fall seriously ill, the chances are very great now that my blood is like this. I have very little energy, and sometimes have to sleep for days on end, so I live one day at a time.

I am not sad that I will die young. I have the feeling that I am not dying. It is true that my body is dying, but I am not. I shall stay. I hope that before I go I will be able to make some contact with the other side so that I will not find that world too strange later on. To put it another

---

* A type of white blood cell which the HIV virus penetrates in order to multiply, finally killing the cell to release the new virus particles.

way, I would like to shake the hand of someone on the other side.

Occasionally, I'm filled with enormous fear about death, and this is because I forget that the earth is round and that life is round as well, that I have died so many times and been reborn. I leave only my body. I am still here and in a while I will have to go on there. Whenever this idea comes to me, I feel peaceful and confident. Sometimes I think that perhaps I have something more important to do there than here, but then I remember there is something I have to do here which I am still waiting for.

For me, the past two years have been very important. In terms of development it doesn't feel like two years, but a lot more than two. I'd never have thought that you could experience such great processes in such a short time. Time is so different from what it was in the past! Before I was HIV positive, I was at a dead point. When I realized I was infected, I felt I started to live. Before, I had been a prisoner of my fears and uncertainties. An enormous burden has been removed from me. Now I have the feeling that I am a person with a right to exist. I feel that I have a basis.

A number of things have been finished, but not quite everything, I did become a Buddy and I think that's very useful. I live one day at a time, more conscious than ever. Everything has acquired a value and a different meaning from in the past. All the events in my life have become meaningful, even difficult ones. I only realize that now. There were many things I had a feeling about before, including the fact that I would die young.

I trust that I will be able to cope with death. I know there will be help from the other side; I have found this in other situations as well. Of course, there will be a struggle. I will not be spared that, but I trust it will be a process of slowly growing towards death. I try to see it as a challenge. In this way it's in my hands, I'm doing something with it and I'm less of a victim. This will be the strength with which I'll fight until I'm ready. There are so many people who die. They are dying this very moment. That's the way it should be, so why shouldn't I be able to cope?

May 1992

After a period of months in which he suffered intense fatigue, fever and coughing attacks, Reinder became very ill last February. He was hospitalized and diagnosed as having AIDS-related pneumonia. When his family from Groningen arrived at his bedside, he had a message for them: "Don't be afraid. I'm not dying yet. I'm not ready for it."

During this final illness he had various "encounters" with "the other side" — animals and monsters which frightened him, his deceased grandmother and uncle who calmed his mind, and a figure of light and love who asked him to step into a boat that was waiting for him. Reinder saw himself as a small frightened boy who was still too afraid to "make the move." He told the figure of light that he was not ready yet. He also saw a very old Chinese man, who radiated great peace and wisdom.

For Reinder these encounters were very real and important. Afraid that his family and nurses thought him crazy, he kept asking, "You believe me, don't you?" I really saw them! I'm not out of my mind!" His mother and sister bought a picture of an old Chinese man for him. "We believe you, Reinder, you're not crazy."

He had hardly recovered from his pneumonia and was just getting used to the idea that he was suffering from AIDS, when within a month the disease struck hard. He became blind in one eye through a viral infection, and to prevent the other eye from going blind as well, he had to lie for hours every day with a drip. He also had problems walking and was advised to use crutches and a wheel-chair when he was allowed to go home. Six weeks later he was hospitalized again with severe symptoms. When after two weeks it appeared that he could not be helped any more, he was taken home according to his wish, where he died peacefully the next day surrounded by family and friends.

He never thought himself as a victim. Again and again he was able to overcome his fear and accept his fate. His incredibly positive strength of mind made it possible for him to fight his battle with dignity and full of confidence, until he was "ready."

On Sunday, July 11, 1993, at six in the evening that moment came.

Soffia (40)

I was born in Panama in 1951. There were four children in our family: three boys and a girl. I was the last but one.

My life has been a series of problems and they began the day I was born. As my mother was giving birth to me, my eight-year-old brother died. Another child deliberately pushed him under a car my brother's teacher was driving. He died of his injuries straightaway.

At first my father, who was a doctor, didn't dare tell my mother — she was staying in the clinic with me — but in the end there was nothing else for it but to tell her.

This event influenced the relationship I had with my mother from the very beginning. In her grief my mother clung onto me. It is as though she transformed the pain in her heart about the loss of her child into love for me. I was her consolation; she needed me for this, I became her dearest child and I have always remained the favourite. We have an indescribably close relationship. For me, my mother has been the most important woman in my life, and the love between us has never changed.

Despite this great love, there were problems in our family which I found very confusing. My parents had a very difficult relationship and they often quarrelled. As I was very dependent on my mother, I always took her side. I used to scream at my father: "Let her go, let her go!" when he hit her. Usually he stopped and went out. I would stay behind with my mother in tears. In fact, I took over the role which the brother who died had had before my birth. When he was still alive he hit my father with the lamp on the bedside table to protect my mother.

There were always two sides in our family; on the one hand, my mother, my dead brother and me, and on the other, my father, my sister and my two other brothers. That's still the case. These sides still exist and will remain beyond death. For example, the grave where my brother is buried is intended for my mother and myself. She won't let anyone else be buried there.

When my mother was pregnant, something else happened which also had a big influence on my life. In Panama, many people are still involved with black magic. They're familiar with magic forces and use them to influence things. My grandmother on my father's side was also involved in this. She hated my mother, probably because she was white, and when my mother was expecting me, she cast a spell to give the baby demonic powers when it was born. I only found this out when I reached adulthood. Although this may sound strange to English ears, this troubled me all my life, as I'll explain later.

I noticed that I was different at a very early age. Even at nursery school I was teased a lot. I was a vulnerable, soft, girlish child, and children are extremely sensitive to others who are different. It's incredible that they could see what adults had not yet perceived.

I hated going to school. For example, I couldn't go to the toilet while I was at school; I always had to restrain myself, because if I went, a group would always follow me. They would throw me on the ground and then start peeing on me. I was regularly attacked, beaten or battered with books.

In countries like Panama, homosexuality is an offence. It's considered very inferior. Boys are real machos. You have to talk and walk in a particularly exaggerated male way, or there's something wrong with you. This was the case as far as I was concerned, and I knew it.

So I did very badly at school and this was reflected in my results. My father found this unacceptable, and he punished me mercilessly. The way in which he punished me would be considered child abuse over here. For example, I had to sit on my knees in the corner. He used to throw corn on the ground beforehand and that really hurt under my knees. Then he would sit behind me with a sort of wooden stick, and as soon as I moved with pain he hit me. He never wondered why I had problems at school, or rather he probably didn't dare to wonder because he could see that I behaved in a girlish way and he forbade me to play with girls. Even my girl cousins were no longer allowed to come to our home or even near to our house or in the same street. He wanted me to be what he expected, and wouldn't accept my girlish behaviour. It irritated him terribly that I sang with a high girlish voice when I took a shower, and that I didn't stand, but sat down on the toilet when I wanted to pee.

At a very young age I had the feeling that I wanted to be a woman. I was simply born in the wrong body and I felt like a woman. When my parents were away, a maid used to let me dress up in her room. She let me wear her clothes and put lipstick on. I thought it was wonderful. It was only when I did that that I felt good. She accepted this in me; there was an unspoken understanding between us. I knew that she would never talk about it.

When I was thirteen I tried to commit suicide. My father had boxes of pills in the library. I could easily get at them and I ate lots. I really didn't want to live any more because I thought I'd have to tell them at home that I felt that I was really a woman. However, anything like that is impossible in our culture and I was particularly afraid that my mother wouldn't love me any more. This had all become such a huge problem for me that in the

end I could only see one way out — and that was to
give up.

When I didn't appear at breakfast the next morning,
they found me in bed unconscious, foaming at the mouth.
When I'd been resuscitated I was treated in my father's
clinic in the psychiatric department. I was only there for
three days, but that was long enough for me to come
across a nurse who was very important to me. She asked
me why I wanted to be Cleopatra — that's what my father
had told her. She was the first person I was able to tell
that I felt like a woman inside, and this was a sort of
liberation. She also told me that to become a woman you
could have injections of female hormones, and that gave
me hope.

When I went home, my mother was there. She held me
in her arms because I was her child and it didn't matter
to her what I was. She only wanted me to be a happy
person. If she hadn't been there, I would have been gone
long ago. From that time, I could always go to her. Her
love just became greater, she understood how difficult it
was for me.

It was different with my father. At that point I became
his enemy and that was how I felt for the rest of my life.
It never went away. He was hard towards me and constantly invented new ways of dealing with me which hurt
me.

For example, he wanted me to have military training.
He had had this training himself and he knew what
happened. It was a residential course and everything
which was seen as being soft in a man became the target
of mockery and aggression. Sometimes it even led to
murder. He told my mother that it would make a man
of me. My mother fought to prevent me from having to
go. She even managed to persuade him to let me go to
Miami, where my sister lived, to follow a hairdressing
course. This was a profession for homosexuals which was

accepted. My mother used all her feminine persuasion, and he was sensitive to it. She won, and I was allowed to leave home.

By now I was sixteen years old and left for Miami. My sister didn't really welcome me and put me out onto the street the very first day. She was terribly ashamed of my feminine appearance and didn't want me to see what she was getting up to either, afraid that I would tell my parents. So I went to live in a student hostel and looked after myself.

In one way it was a wonderful time, and I was free. But in America it's also illegal for a man to dress as a woman. I had beautiful long hair — very feminine — and in the daytime I wore a man's wig. No one noticed this; even my mother never noticed when I used to visit her.

At home, and when I went out, I wore my hair loose and I wore women's clothes; then I was myself. But as a result I came into contact with a world which was completely new to me, a really hard world. The police often chased us out of discotheques because we were "dressed up." They would spit in our faces and roughly scrub the make-up from our faces with paper they picked up on the street. If you were unlucky they would take you to the police station and keep you there for a while, humiliating you. But several times they took me to a quiet spot and forced me to have sex with them. Then they would take everything from me and throw me out of the car leaving me to find my way back as best I could.

As a transsexual you have the lowest rights, or even worse — no rights at all. You're less than nothing. This is because people become very confused: they see a woman, often an extremely feminine woman, and when they hear that you're a man they feel deceived. They're unable to rely on their judgment and this makes them aggressive;

the animal in them gets the better of them and unfortunately I was a victim of this many times.

When I was seventeen, I started to live as a woman. I wore dresses and frocks and felt much freer. A doctor gave a friend of mine and me female hormones so that my voice was higher and I developed a bust. Meanwhile, we were doing dangerous things. We were able to obtain these female hormones illegally, and simply injected each other with them in the street. No one knew what was the right dosage and we didn't care. We wanted to be women, and that was the important thing. I also had my beard removed with electrolysis.

I loved going to college. There were other people there like me, they understood me, and that was a relief. I studied to become a beautician as well as a hairdresser and there was a salon attached to the college. Many women like to go to homosexual hairdressers because they seem to make good listeners. In that way I got to know the life of the whole city as a hairdresser. You were almost a psychiatrist. My customers really liked me. I never had any complaints about my work, and there were always people queuing up for me to cut their hair.

I stayed in Miami for four years. I passed my diplomas and learned to live in a world which I had never heard of: a world in which money, sex and power seemed to be the most important things on earth; a world for which my education had not prepared me. It was a world full of hatred and demonic forces, while my mother had raised me to be good and give love to people.

Three times I narrowly escaped being murdered. This may sound unbelievable to many people, but it's really true. Twice I was almost strangled, and the other time it was a crazy man with a gun who was forcing me to have sex with him. The first attempt was in Miami, the other two in Germany. These were very shocking experiences for me, but it was still easier for me than to live life as a man.

I was taken away from Miami by my father when I had got into great difficulties by mistake. A nice man treated a girlfriend and me to a drink in a café. He asked us to go out with him, and we thought it'd be fun. To cut a long story short, we were surrounded by police cars on the way. It turned out that this man was one of a gang who had committed a murder just before we met him. We immediately became suspects. I was in prison for about two months before the trial. This was a terrible time. I was put in a cell with the homosexuals. In itself, this was safer than with the men; I may have been a man, but I would certainly have been mistreated by them. Quite a lot went on with the homosexuals as well. At night the guards would regularly come and point out someone they wanted to have sex with. If you refused, you would be mistreated and I was often the one they chose. I was the most feminine of the group and I certainly knew it. Once I was even sold by a guard to a prisoner in another cell for the night. In America it's terrible to be in jail.

It was very bad for me to leave my friend behind in jail. We had an alibi, because we were both with the beautician at the time the murder was committed. They never checked that. We were only transsexuals. I was released because the witnesses were sure that there hadn't been a woman at the murder. My friend was wearing jeans that day and a black leather jacket, just like one of the murderers ... She was given nine years.

When my father brought me home my mother was able to accept me as a woman. She told me that if I had been a girl I would have been called Soffia Isobel. This is what I later called myself. My father was shocked by my feminine appearance.

Shortly afterwards, I left for Paris. There I did an advanced hairdressing course and trained as a beautician, but in the end I couldn't find any work anyway. First of all, they'd say yes when they saw me, but when I showed them my papers and they saw that I was actually a man, they would say no. They said they couldn't do it because of the customers. It was sheer hypocrisy — they simply meant that they were put off or something.

Anyway, I was forced to find work in a nightclub. Many of my friends became prostitutes but I didn't want to do that. I wanted my self-respect. I was not a whore! But there were situations where I had no choice; for example, when I had no money left for food. Fortunately, this didn't happen very often. I learned belly-dancing and all sorts of other dances from different cultures. I made my own clothes and worked on a contractual basis for nightclubs. This went very well for a long time. I danced in Switzerland, Germany, Albania, Beirut, Holland and so on. Sometimes I danced for princes and sultans in Kuwait and for a long time I earned good money. I had to work very hard and it was always at night, but I didn't mind.

While I was living in France, I went to America for an operation to be given real breasts. They do this with silicon. To give my masculine appearance a more rounded look, the silicon was also injected into my face and in my hips. I was very satisfied because I had become a beautiful woman.

Many women have an operation to remove the penis and make a vagina. Initially I wanted this operation as well. I had already paid for it. It was going to be done in Germany and it would cost £4,500. My mother was paying for it because she knew how important it was to me. Just before the operation I thought about it again. In fact, 98% of my girlfriends who had had this operation had committed suicide after a time. After the operation they

84

imagined that they were one hundred per cent female, but that's not really true. You are, and always will be a transsexual, and so after the operation you're a trans- sexual who has had an operation. My girlfriends were always afraid of not being feminine enough or of being discovered. The other thing is that after the operation you no longer have any sexual feelings, which many people deny, but that's simply how it is. All these things together made them so depressed that they decided to opt out.

Then I thought: Soffia, a man cannot make a woman, only God can do that, and so I decided not to have the operation after all. The doctor never gave me my money back and I didn't dare to tell my mother that I didn't have the operation because her money was gone. She thinks I've had the operation but I haven't. I am a man below the waist and a woman above it. I have completely accepted myself as I am and have kept my self-esteem, despite all the humiliation and indignity that I've suffered. Some- times people threw stones at me because I was different. Obviously I reacted to this. I'm not someone who simply looks on in a long-suffering way, but I knew that this was part of my fate. It was another thing I had to accept, or I would simply have had to adapt to my destiny as a man. It's important in life not to lose your self-esteem.

Most transsexuals become criminals. They get kicked down and humiliated so often that they don't know any better. In many cases they haven't been happy at home either. But I didn't want to become involved in their cri- minal activities. When I saw that someone was in danger of becoming their victim, I immediately tried to prevent it, even when the consequences could lead to great difficul- ties. For example, five of us went to America to have silicon injections. I returned to France the next day. The others stayed a week longer to see America. When they came back, I found out that they'd stolen tubs of silicon, and two of them gave various people injections and charged a lot of money, though they didn't know what they were doing.

One of them had already had injections in her face from a doctor in France but wanted more injections to get it to look rounder. The next day she couldn't move a muscle in her face. She could only just open her mouth. She complained to the doctor who'd done the first treatment and demanded her money back. I thought this was scandalous, because I knew that he'd be struck off for it, even though he was innocent. I appeared as a defence witness to tell the truth and I knew that from then on, it was war for me. The doctor was acquitted, and the plaintiff went to prison, but I was no longer safe. These were Brazilian transsexuals, so they were men with a man's strength. Whenever they saw me in the street they'd shout: "There's Soffia," and then they'd beat me up. Often they beat me so badly that they left me unconscious.

Once I was helped by a stranger who fought them for me. He took me home half dead, and looked after me until I had regained my strength. Without laying a finger on me, he took me back to my flat five days later. I often think about that, a stranger who did something like that for me.

I lived in Paris in an apartment complex with eight hundred transsexuals and when I became aware of all the criminal activities which were going on there, I was so shocked that I moved to a safer place. It took me a long time before I really saw the evil, although I lived in the middle of it. At first, I really didn't see it. I was very naive. My mother had never told me about the evil in the world and so I was unable to recognize it. That's really how it is: if you don't know it's there, you don't see it. But while I was in that flat my eyes were opened.

When I look back at my life in the nightclubs, I think that I did some beautiful shows, just as I used to imagine in my dreams in the past. It was wonderful. I always loved seeing people having fun and helping them to enjoy themselves. Laughing faces have always made me happy. I introduced a new element into the showy world of striptease. I didn't strip for the sensuality of it like my colleagues, but for the pleasure of it, and the dancing.

If I'd been born different, I'd have liked to do the same thing in another profession — to give people pleasure and bring them happiness. But because of my transsexuality, I was only able to do it in that particular world.

I have always been persecuted, always been running away, always abused. I was forced to do things with men which were deeply humiliating, and that was worst in Holland. In Holland I had no rights. I was an illegal immigrant and they took advantage of it. For example, I was forced to work in a nightclub for a pittance with a forged contract and to do things with men which I really hated. But what else could I do, where else could I go? I couldn't go back to Panama. I was a woman with breasts but I had a man's passport. I would have been arrested at the border straightaway.

I went to Holland because I had to flee from Germany where I had lived before. I had had a relationship with a man which had gone badly wrong. I was on my own, lonely, looking for warmth and love when I met him. I trusted him, fell in love, and thought that I had finally found what I was looking for; I became completely dependent on him. However, he abused me dreadfully and completely undressed me in a metaphorical sense. Time after time I believed his stories of regret and repentance and he would be so good to me that I could no longer resist. In retrospect, I think he was the one who infected me with the HIV virus. I didn't know it at the time, but later on I realized that he must have known, because he sometimes told me that he knew he would die young. In fact, he's dead now.

One day he stole money from my bank account and threw my clothes out of the window into the snow. As I was sitting in the snow amongst my clothes, crying and in terrible distress, something happened which always happens when I reach a very low point in my life. From nowhere a stranger came up to me and asked if he could help me. She was also a transsexual. She helped me to gather my clothes and I went to live with her for a short while. When she saw how easily my friend, who soon traced me, influenced me, she took me to Holland where I lost track of her again.

In my life so many terrible things have happened which ordinary people would not believe. What I'm telling you here is only a fragment, and for some people it may seem incredible, but for me it's the real world.

Because of my nature I was forced against my better judgment to live in a world of sex and drugs. I never touched drugs, although almost everyone around me was on them. And the strange thing is that I don't have many sexual inclinations at all. I like hugs and cuddles, but that's really all I want. In every situation I've always tried to do the right thing and to be a good person. My mother was always an example for me. Although I haven't seen her for twenty-six years, she gave me the strength to live in this way.

For example, I was once robbed by a junkie who was sleeping in my house because he didn't have a home. The next day I saw him in a bar. I went up to him and warmly offered him a drink. He looked at me disbelievingly to see whether I meant it, and I really did mean it. He turned bright red but I was truly sincere. I didn't want to repay evil with evil, but balance the evil with good.

That's what I've always tried to do in my life. Whenever

someone did something terrible to me, I always tried to show that person that the world doesn't consist only of bad people. Even when I was abused, I tried to balance this with something good and that was necessary quite a few times.

I'm sure that this was also because of my grandmother's black magic and the curse she had put on me. That was the reason why I became super-sensitive to evil, so that I learnt to recognize it sooner and sooner. Moreover, there was one thing she hadn't counted on, and that was that I was a Christian. I am a child of God and whenever I came across evil I'd say, sometimes out loud: "You can't get me, I'm not yours, I am God's. Jesus is with me."

Often it was very difficult to fight these forces because I actually see these creatures. At night, I always have nightmares. Ever since I can remember, I've seen monsters in my dreams lying in wait for me. I have terrible fights at night and often wake up screaming. But I know that fear makes you weaker. Fear gives them strength and so I say the Lord's Prayer, read the Bible or tell them that they can't get me because I belong to God. This calms me down. I'm convinced that I am a child of God because whenever there was no way out, help would appear from nowhere, from a stranger on my path, who'd help me so I could go on.

Once I had a very strange experience. This was in Amsterdam. I was going home from work at night, walking in the street on my own. I had terrible worries and couldn't think of any solution to them. I felt desperate. Suddenly I saw a man walking straight towards me and there was no one else around to be seen. I thought this was going to be a big problem, especially as he was coming straight towards me. I tried to avoid him, but he came closer and closer and didn't move aside to the left or right. It was as though he wanted to walk straight through me and I felt very frightened. Then, when he was very close to me, he

placed his hands on my shoulder and said in Spanish, my
mother tongue: "Don't be afraid, I'll always look after
you." In Spanish in Amsterdam! I stood still in astonish-
ment, and when I looked round, there was no one to be
seen. For a moment I was completely at sea and I wondered how anyone could look after me if they didn't know
me. My friend said that it must have been an angel, but
when I think of an angel I think of a child with wings, not
of an apparition. But it must have been something like
that. Who else could have helped me?

All my life I've had supernatural feelings and seen
things, but this really amazed me. It's very strange that I
can't remember the face at all.

Shortly after this, I met Tony, the man I've been living
with for eight years. He also came to me like a saviour
when I was in great need. I was moving house, and everything was packed up. I'd seen the new house and had
been given the key on the day I moved. When I arrived at
the house with all my things in the car, it turned out that
the owner had rented it to friends two days before. I was
desperate and was sitting on the pavement in tears, when
Tony came up to me and asked me what the matter was.
I explained the situation to him and he said that I could
use his room for a while. He had a two-roomed flat. He
slept on the sofa.

That's how it has been for eight years. Tony and I have
a brother and sister relationship. He has never made
sexual advances to me. He's my best friend. At that time
I didn't know that I was infected with the HIV virus. By
now, I have already had AIDS for almost four years.

A year before I was diagnosed as having AIDS, I was
sitting at home one evening when I suddenly saw a figure
walking past my window — I live three stories up —
calling me. It was a man, but I couldn't see his face.
He was walking very slowly, and looked at me once
and suddenly I knew that he was Death. In my fright I

started to pray and said to Tony: "Tony, I've just seen Death!" He told me not to be such an idiot because he doesn't believe in these things at all. But from that time I knew that there was something waiting for me. I saw it as a sign that my time was up. I said to Tony: "I've been warned."

When I was taken into hospital a year later with pneumonia, and I was told I had AIDS, I was not thrown off balance for a moment. I was able to accept it from the very first moment. I'm not afraid of death at all. Perhaps this is something to do with our culture; death is part of it. Why should I be afraid? I believe in God and in Heaven. I've had a very difficult and lonely life, and I've always had the feeling that I don't belong here on Earth. I'm going back to where I belong, why should I be sad about that? I don't belong here, and my time has come. I accept that my path goes where it goes. I'm not exactly counting the days. I'm going on doing what I can, not what I want. I want many things but I can only do very few. I have gone from one extreme, as a dancer in the biggest and best-known nightclubs throughout the world, to the other, in my bed in our flat. Apart from my Buddies I no longer see anyone. Everyone who called himself a friend, has let me go. I am not complaining — that's how it is, and I accept it. I use my strength to endure my sick bed with as much dignity as I can.

Since my earliest youth I have felt drawn to Egyptian culture. If there is such a thing as reincarnation, I was an Egyptian in a previous life. I visited that country and studied the language of the hieroglyphics. Everything was familiar to me there. I expected to find my own grave there, but that didn't happen.

It may sound strange, but if I did live there, I was a Pharaoh. I'm sure of that. I have regal feelings inside me and often have images of a nation obeying and working for me. Sometimes, when things aren't going very well, memories come back to me. I also have the feeling that I could govern a country on the basis of honesty and sincerity. I'd only do those things that were good for the population. It really hurts me when I see what rulers can do to their people. Perhaps it was because I was a Pharaoh that I'm not afraid of death now. If I died before and have been reborn, I must have some knowledge of the other side. Something inside me tells me that what's coming is good, and that I'm going where I belong. Perhaps people think I'm imagining things; anyway, that's how it is for me.

Two years before I became ill, I painted the story of my life on the walls of my room in Egyptian hieroglyphics. I lie here and feel at home. I have one more wish and I've started working on it. I would like to paint my coffin with Egyptian pictures. It's standing next to my bed; painting it is a slow process because I am very ill. While the coffin remains unfinished I can't die, though if that's how it must be, that's how it will be.

I try to bear the pain as much as possible because dying is painful. Many people ask for an injection so that they can die quickly. They forget that Christ also suffered terribly for us. I've talked to the doctors about my wishes: I don't want an injection to end my life, but there must be no intervention either to prolong it. When God says: "Your time has come," that will have to be the end. And that's what I'm waiting for.

I have agreed with my Buddies that they will lay me out when I die. I don't want anyone else to see the proof of the fact that I was a man. It's because of that that I've suffered so much in my life, and I can't bear the thought that they might laugh about me. That's why I hope to die at home.

On earth I did what I had to do, and that's why it was easy to say goodbye. It's very difficult for me to leave my mother behind. Parents ought to go first, not the other way round. My father has known for a long time that I'm ill. He has been to Holland several times and has paid for my cremation and the Requiem Mass. I noticed that he was full of guilt feelings. Obviously he wanted to make amends for what he'd done to me, but it's too late for that now. Not that I hate him, I don't feel that, but I'm no longer able to love him. I just feel very sorry for him.

My mother has only known for a few months. We can only talk to each other on the telephone because she's afraid of flying, and I haven't been able to visit Panama for twenty-six years because I'd be put in prison. She cried on the telephone when I told her. She said she wanted to die as well on the day that I die. But I said to her: "Mother, you're so old, only a little longer and we'll meet again. You don't have to wait very long." That helped a little but not much. For myself, I'm looking forward to the three of us being in heaven together: my mother, my brother and me.

April 1992

In the last week of May there was an unexpected telephone call from Panama. Soffia's mother phoned to say that in a few days time she would take the plane to Holland with her husband. Her longing to see Soffia once more before her death had overcome her great fear of flying. She begged her daughter to wait and not die before she'd seen her. Perhaps she felt there wasn't much time left.

Soffia wept with happiness. She simply couldn't take it in that after twenty-six years she would be seeing and holding her mother within a few days. At her request, she was quickly admitted to hospital for another blood transfusion, in the hope that this would give her some strength.

Four days later her mother arrived. Their reunion was indescribable, and apart from one time when she went out for something to eat, her mother stayed by Soffia's bedside for nine days. It was moving to see how devotedly and lovingly she looked after Soffia.

In the nine days that her mother was there, Soffia said several times that Death, the man in black whom she had seen walking by the window a year before her AIDS diagnosis, was present in the room. "It's different now from that time, because then it was frightening. Now it's good, it's a good death," she told me.

It was difficult for them when Soffia's mother had to leave. They were both very sad, but whenever her mother said that they would never see each other again, Soffia reminded her sternly: "Mother, you mustn't say that. We shall see each other with God. I'll wait for you there and we'll soon be together again. Don't cry about my death, it's good that I'm going."

On the day that her mother left — it was a Tuesday — Soffia was also starting to leave. She slept a lot, became confused, and kept speaking French instead of Dutch. In the following days she sank further and further away and moments of lucidity became increasingly rare.

Those days were used for being together and completing the Egyptian pictures which Soffia had painted on her coffin. In clear moments she was even able to give some instructions. The result was splendid.

On Friday evening the priest of the Christian Community gave her the last rites as she had wished. On Monday morning, June 15, at ten minutes past twelve, less than a week after her mother's departure, she fell asleep quietly. As agreed, she was laid out by Tony and one of her buddies and the coffin was sealed straightaway.

She stayed at home in her beautiful coffin in her Egyptian room, and we guarded over her until the funeral took place. The atmosphere was peaceful.

Her father and sister came over to be present at the cremation. They told us that Soffia's mother had accepted her death quietly. She had said that this was because Soffia had been able to convince her that it was not necessary to cry, because she was certain that she would be happy with God. This was a source of consolation to her.

June 1992

Maria (36)

I was born the oldest in a family of three children. I had two younger brothers so I was the only girl. After my younger brother was born, my mother suffered from rheumatism. She was only twenty-four years old and her illness became increasingly serious as her life went on. When I think back to my youth, I could say that I had a good time at home until puberty. My parents looked after us well and I got on fine with them. The atmosphere at home was good, and I felt safe.

I was a good and happy child and always joined in everything. I liked playing with boys best — I thought girls were sissies, but I was attracted by the adventurous and wild games that boys play. I was quite a wild kid myself and liked to play out in the street a lot.

When I was six, something happened which is still a problem to me now. Our family had rented a holiday home. My parents became friends with the people who had the house next to us and we did lots of things together in the holidays. When the holidays came to an end, it was arranged that I could go and stay with this "aunt and uncle." I got on very well with their little boy and they thought I was sweet.

One day when I was there, the aunt went shopping. I stayed behind on my own with the uncle and he abused me. I was very shocked but he threatened me with all sorts of things if I told my parents what had happened. For example, he said I could go to prison and might never be allowed to go back to my parents. It made me very scared and I never said anything about it to my parents but I did start to feel very guilty. I thought that if I could go to prison for that, it must have been my own fault.

I went to stay there several times. The aunt would ask if I'd like to come and I didn't dare to say no, because I was afraid that I would have to say why I didn't want to go and I couldn't do that. When I went to stay again I was very frightened and whenever I was there I hoped that the aunt wouldn't have to go away anywhere. But the uncle managed to get her to go every time, and he would take me again. This happened several times over a period of about two years. Although they didn't know why, my parents realized after a while that I didn't like going there, and so I didn't have to go again.

It was only when I was twenty and had sexual problems with my boyfriend because of these experiences that I told my father. He thought it was terrible that I'd been afraid to talk about it before and understood the problems that I had with my boyfriend very well. I only told my mother about it ten years later, but she didn't believe me and she said I had an overactive imagination. That hurt me a lot, but I simply repressed my feelings, as I usually did.

While I was at primary school my life was reasonably quiet and happy. Everything went smoothly in those days. I didn't much like going up to the secondary school. You're no longer one of the little ones, but you aren't accepted either by the older children. Fortunately, this changed completely when I was in the second year. You might say that the sweet little girl I had been was completely transformed. I have to admit that I turned into a real brat.

There were two groups in our class — the girls who were boy-mad, and the troublemakers. I felt particularly attracted to the latter. We really got up to no good together and I gave some of the teachers a very hard time.

I soon made a name for myself and sometimes I was automatically blamed for things — which I obviously didn't accept.

In any case, I didn't move up to the third year because I failed some of my subjects, and then it happened again the next year. Normally you're only allowed to repeat a year once, but as I got good marks for my main subjects, I was allowed to repeat the year again. Unfortunately, this was a waste of time. So I left school at sixteen without any qualifications. At home, I was also very difficult. I disagreed with everything, thought my parents were boring and bourgeois and told them several times that my friends' parents were much better than they were. It seemed to me that my girlfriends were allowed to do anything and I was jealous of their freedom. For example, their parents allowed them to go to a particular bar where I wasn't allowed to go. Once I pretended that I was going to bed early, but disappeared secretly through the window and went anyway. My father realized what I was doing, and was waiting for me in front of the bar in his car. Obviously this led to terrible trouble.

I turned everything into a problem. If I had to wash up or do anything else at home, I was furious about it, and this constantly led to conflict. In retrospect, this makes me feel really ashamed because I see now that my parents were actually doing quite a good job. Sometimes I think that my own children will be allowed to do less than I was allowed to, but that's talking with hindsight.

When I repeated the second year for the second time I was fourteen, and there was a group of children who were already using a lot of dope and cocaine. I didn't smoke any myself, but I was strongly attracted to the feeling that these people belonged together and no one could do anything to them.

In the swimming pool where I often went, I met someone who lived in a squat who told me that she had a boat where they had a really good time. Out of curiosity I went to have a look with a girl in my class. Soon I was one of the regular visitors to that boat. Everyone who went there used drugs — mostly hard drugs — and for a long time I tried to get them off the drugs. I was the only one who didn't use any, and I was worried about the others because I could see that they couldn't do without, and that all their money went on drugs. But they didn't really listen to me, and so at a certain point I stopped trying to convince them.

My parents knew about the existence of this place and what was going on there. They were very worried about me, and my father took me away from the boat several times, but of course that didn't help at all. I just went my own way and I wasn't prepared to listen to my parents at all. I was very rebellious and I wanted to be free. I found a kind of freedom on the boat. There was a very friendly atmosphere; you were always welcome there, and that gave me a sense of having my own space where I could be myself. I was accepted by the people there and this gave me self-confidence. When I was fifteen, I had my first boyfriend and it seemed quite normal to go to bed with him.

When I left school I started working in an administrative office. I liked that a lot. I liked working, and I had a very nice set of colleagues. By that time I had a steady boyfriend and I wanted to live with him. I realized that my parents wouldn't give me permission because I was only sixteen years old.

One evening I packed my suitcase and hid it under the bed. In the morning, I left with my suitcase without them seeing me. I handed it to my boyfriend at his house, and then I simply went on to my work as though nothing had happened. It was three days later when I rang my parents to tell them I wasn't going back home.

Obviously they weren't exactly over the moon when they heard. They didn't agree with it at all and thought it was stupid, but by now they'd found out that they couldn't influence me. I didn't give them a choice. The fact that they left it at that, meant that I was able to stay in contact with them. If they hadn't accepted it, I would certainly have broken all contact with them. So I was able to go back home after a period when there had been a distance between us and I'm very grateful to my parents for their attitude at that time. Everything they warned me about happened. I found out through my own experience, but it was a hard way to learn.

My boyfriend was a drug addict. At first we had quite a good time together, but sometimes he got aggressive. It was very gradual; he'd hit me once and then again, and afterwards he was always very sorry. But it happened more and more often, and in the end he was beating me up regularly. Sometimes I'd have a black eye, sometimes I was covered in bruises. I lied to my parents, telling them I'd knocked myself. In retrospect, I sometimes wonder how I managed to take all this, but it was such a gradual process and I kept thinking that things would get better. But they never did.

At first I didn't use any drugs myself, and I was always the only one in the group who didn't join in. One day I gave in. There were two reasons why I tried it. I was fat and I wanted to lose weight. They told me that speed and amphetamines made you lose weight. The other reason was that I could see that everyone who used drugs felt wonderful, and because of my boyfriend's aggression, I certainly didn't feel wonderful myself.

I wanted to feel wonderful too. So I gave in to temptation and soon became part of a group of regular users. I certainly lost weight — in fact, I was all skin and bones — and I soon couldn't do without the drugs. My friend was on such heavy doses that he was always out of money. He started to put pressure on me because he wanted me to become a prostitute for him. This was despite the fact that I had big sexual problems because of the child abuse I had suffered.

Meanwhile, his aggression had become so serious that I even ended up in hospital once because I had internal bleeding in my head after he hit me. I was very scared of him, but that wasn't the worst of it. By now, my mother was in a wheelchair because of her rheumatoid arthritis, and my boyfriend threatened to hurt her if I refused to work for him. I was really afraid because he was quite capable of doing it.

In the end, I made my first arrangement with a man. I was in fear and trembling. I left crying my eyes out and came back still crying, but then he just sent me out again. Fortunately my feelings were dulled by the drugs, and after a while I even started to get used to the work.

My boyfriend went to prison several times for theft. While he was inside I stopped being a prostitute straight-away because I only did it when he made me. In retro-spect, I think I could easily have left him then, but the strange thing is that once you're in that situation, you start to accept that life, and it becomes your reality. Leaving home, where you feel familiar, is a big step, and when you're young you always think that everything will be alright. Anyway, I was really crazy about that boy. Meanwhile I was also injecting drugs though I didn't dare to do it myself and always got somebody else to do it for me.

When he was back in prison yet again, I put up a friend of his because he asked me to. His friend was a very unstable person who was constantly in and out of psychi-atric care. When I'd had enough of him and told him that he had to go away, he injected me with an overdose of heroin. I didn't know he'd given me an overdose, and lost consciousness immediately.

By coincidence — but after all, what is coincidence? — another friend came round and rang the police. By the time the ambulance arrived my heart had already stopped, but they resuscitated me and brought me back to life. They were certainly quite rough about it because after I left intensive care, my chest was black and blue all over. After this, I'd really had enough of things. I decided to leave my boyfriend's circle for good and had the strength to do it. I moved to a secret address, and when he left jail the bird had flown.

Meanwhile, my younger brother had also become a drug addict. He'd kept this a secret from me for a long time, but eventually I found out anyway. This was terrible for my parents. Having two addicted children is no joke. My father was still trying to protect me from all sorts of things. Whenever he saw my car standing where he thought there might be trouble, he'd simply take me away, but I never really listened to him. Looking back, that was a real shame.

What I appreciated so much in him was that every time he trusted me. Sometimes I borrowed money from him and told him it was for methadone to help me kick the habit, but I secretly bought drugs with it. He knew that I would do this but trusted me again and again. Then I would feel really guilty and try even harder to come off drugs.

Drugs killed my brother. He only lived to be twenty-four. In fact, I still haven't come to terms with his death. He was my favourite brother. Even when we were very small we always stood up for each other, and we loved each other a great deal. He had been given a mixture of heroin and some other drug by a friend. After he had smoked it, he had problems walking. At that time he was living with me and I could see that there was something wrong straightaway. I immediately went to our parents with him and they telephoned the doctor. He was taken into casualty and died in hospital three weeks later.

His death was a terrible blow for my parents. The fact that it was a consequence of taking drugs made it even worse. They didn't tell the family because it was a secret from the outside world. My mother in particular didn't want anyone to know.

My parents never came to terms with his death; it still really upsets them. As for myself, I felt a great deal of anger and rage after his death. I kept thinking, why him and not my other brother? I couldn't get on with him at all. Now I think that it was terribly mean, but I did think it very often.

I couldn't feel real sadness about his death because my feelings were locked away. I have the idea that this was because of the time when I was abused by my "uncle." That's when something really went wrong with me; since then my feelings have been imprisoned. The only thing I can feel about everything that happened in my life is a terrible rage, but I keep it under control. I feel that accidents could happen if I really let go. At the very least, the chairs would be flying through the windows and that would be too much. What I do — and what I've always done — is to turn to drugs or drink. That helps me keep going in this life, otherwise I'd go crazy. Drink makes everything easier.

After a while I came across a girlfriend who was still a prostitute. I was working in a bank myself and was really getting on quite well. However, drugs remained a problem for me. Because of her, I went back to prostitution. I was living two lives; a respectable life at the bank, and in the evening I was a prostitute.

This time the step to prostitution was easier. I had become used to earning a lot of money and it was pleasant to be wanted and always be given a lot of money. While a colleague earned fifty guilders, I would get two hundred; and the attention of the clients gave me a sense of importance. Moreover, the atmosphere amongst the prostitutes made me feel good. I was completely accepted and trusted by them and the solidarity amongst us was very strong.

I had other relationships with men several times but every time it went wrong. I would always end up with someone who abused me in one way or another, or beat me up. Until I met my husband. He came from the country to Amsterdam to try "it" just once. He was a sweet and shy man and I fell in love with him straightaway. Three days later we moved in together.

Gradually I gave up prostitution and I was finding it easier and easier to stay away from drugs. However, I did start drinking much more instead. After just over a year I was pregnant, and a few months before the birth of my son we got married. That was in 1986.

My son was born five weeks premature and weighed only five pounds. After four weeks an observant paediatrician gave him a sort of methadone to cure him of his addiction because he cried so much. They didn't discuss this with me which I thought very stupid because I hadn't really used many drugs during my pregnancy. But the doctor said that he was addicted. When he was allowed to come home after five weeks, I stopped giving him the medicine straightaway and there were no problems; he was very quiet. From time to time I had a drink problem. Sometimes I'd go for a long time without any drink, but as soon as something happened which affected me emotionally, things went wrong again.

Exactly two years later, I had a little girl. She was a week premature, but she still weighed seven pounds. Everything went very well with her. When I was admitted to hospital last year to stop drinking I told the doctors that I had been feeling terribly tired for a long time. I was washed out and everything I did was an enormous effort. Because they were aware of my history with drugs, they asked if they could also do an HIV test. Without thinking about it I gave my consent.

When I went back for the result after I'd been discharged the doctor asked me how things were going with my drinking. I said that things were going well, but that I had given in just once. He answered: "In that case you spent four weeks here for nothing, and furthermore you're infected with HIV."

I was furious about the way in which he told me this. I hadn't prepared myself for that result at all. I was completely overwhelmed and could only keep going with drink. Immediately afterwards I had my children tested and my husband had a test as well. Thank God, they're not infected, and I'm really glad about that because I really couldn't have borne it.

I must have become infected before I met my husband. If it was an infected needle, that must have been about ten years ago. But it could also have been the result of having sex with a drug addict before my marriage. In that case, it was about eight or nine years ago.

In retrospect, I realize that I've been extremely tired ever since the birth of my son. I could never put my finger on why this was. I regularly had a home help, because I simply couldn't cope with the housekeeping. After the result I was terribly afraid and rebellious. I thought I'd die very quickly and that I'd therefore have to let my children go. I was also afraid to be a burden to my husband because of my illness. That's why I took all my sleeping pills. I thought I might as well go straightaway so they would be rid of me. However, when it looked as though it might be my children who found me, and not my husband, I told them what I'd done and I had my stomach pumped.

Initially, my drinking problem became much worse when I found out that I was HIV positive. Recently I was admitted to a convalescent centre for six weeks to calm down. They tried to tackle my drinking problem there. I would like to stop drinking and lead a healthy life so that I can stay with my children as much as possible. Drinking just accelerates the process. Recently I've started taking tablets which make me sick if I start drinking. I hope that they'll help me to give up. I've also given my bank card to my husband so that I can't get any money to buy drink. I really mean it, I want to stop.

In the convalescent centre they also looked at everything that happened to me in the past. I now realize that things went wrong with me because of my experience of child abuse. That only really came out in adolescence when I rebelled against everything. It was my childhood experience which made me lose confidence in everything. I still haven't really come to terms with it, or with everything that happened afterwards. I can't express myself at all; I can't share my feelings about everything that has happened to me, but I am gradually losing my feelings of guilt about all that. A child isn't guilty of something like that.

But still, I have plenty of other guilt feelings. After all, it's my own fault that I started drinking so much and that I'm HIV positive. I can get very angry with myself.

I'm starting to get used to the fact that I'm HIV positive. I try to think about dying as little as possible, but there are days when that doesn't work. The thoughts go round and round my head all day. I'm still afraid — not afraid of death, but afraid of losing my children. It's worst for them. Obviously it's a terrible thing for my husband as well, but he's a good, sweet man; I'm sure that he'll find another wife after a while. It's different for my children. I am their mother and you only have one mother. No one else can ever take that place, no matter how well she does it. I can't bear the thought of letting them go. That's what makes me so afraid. Sometimes I start panicking. I refuse to think that it will happen quickly. I keep telling myself that I was born on Whit Sunday, and that's a good sign, I've survived so many things, I'll just live to be sixty. But it continues to gnaw at me because really I know better. I live between fear and hope; sometimes one wins out, sometimes the other.

It's a big problem doing the housework and looking after the children. I have too little energy. I want to use all the strength I have for them, but sometimes it's difficult even to get them dressed and take them to school, because when I wake up, I feel exhausted. The housework just doesn't get done, there's chaos everywhere, but fortunately I'll have help with that soon. My children are all that matters to me. If they need me, I want to be there for them. They're the only things in my life that really belong to me and I really want to bring them up myself.

My husband's sister has promised to look after my children when things get to that point. We made an agreement. I don't really talk to my husband about death. I don't think he's able to. He keeps saying: "Lead a healthy life, then things won't be so bad." But one day he'll know better.

I don't talk to my parents about it either. I can talk to my father best. I'm like him and I love him a lot, but we don't talk about dying. It's too difficult. It's also difficult to live with the uncertainty. For example, I'd find it easier to know that I had another six months left. You can prepare yourself for that, but not knowing when the end will come is very draining.

I often wonder why this happened to me. I've been abused all my life. At last I have a loving husband who is faithful to me and two lovely children, and now this. Why?

I grew up in the Reformed Church and had my children baptized. But I don't believe in God. I think I lost my faith a long time ago. If there were a God, surely he wouldn't have allowed everything that happened to me.

I've decided for myself that when I become dependent, I want an injection. Euthanasia seems the best way, because I don't want to be a burden to my husband and children.

For me, dead is dead, finished, all over ... the end of it, all over. And yet ... very occasionally, I have the feeling that my brother who died is here with me. It's as though he's warning me. "Watch out, Marie!" he says, but I suppose it's only my imagination. If it were possible for me to contact my children after my death, I wouldn't want that anyway. They have to go on and I wouldn't like to come between them and the new mother they might have.

I hope so much that they have a better life than I did. But what a lot of fuss I'm making, I'm staying with them. I refuse to die. I'll live to be sixty and that's the end of it!

June 1992

Paul (24)

The circumstances in which I was born can only really be understood if I start by saying something about my mother's youth.

My mother grew up in Liverpool. Her parents were gypsies. Her mother was an alcoholic and her father went to prison for murder. As a result, she grew up without any love, and when she was twelve she got into trouble with the law. When the police went to see her mother, she didn't want to look after her daughter any more, and so my mother ended up in a women's jail until she was nineteen because there were no youth prisons at the time.

Because of all these experiences, she started taking drugs at a very early age. Her only support was a sister whom she loved very much, but she was in prison as well. They kept in contact by writing letters and were a great support to each other in that way.

After coming out of prison she met my father, married him and went to live in the same street as her sister.

My parents both took drugs, so I was born to addicted parents. I was their second child, and after me there was another brother. We were three boys.

I was born two months premature. I was very small and had respiratory problems, so my life began in an incubator. I don't know if this had anything to do with my mother's drug habit; I never asked her.

My earliest memory is when I wasn't quite three years old. We were still living in England and I can picture the street where we lived and where I played with my cousin. It was fun.

When I was three, we ran away from England because
my father had big tax debts. He had friends in Holland
who had somewhere for us to live, and so we went there.
I distinctly remember arriving there by car.

We settled illegally in Amsterdam and lived on a house-
boat belonging to my father's friends. My father started
drug dealing to make a living. He was dealing hashish, so
he wasn't home very much. My mother didn't see him
very much. He was usually in bars and only came home
late at night.

Just after we came to Holland, my mother's sister died
in England. She had had an asthma attack and had not
been able to start breathing again. This was terrible for
my mother because her sister was very important to her.
They had a very close relationship, and after her sister's
death my mother really started using a lot of hard drugs.
She began using heroin and things rapidly started to go
downhill.

At a certain point both my parents decided they wanted
to stop using drugs and each of them separately turned
to friends. When they had managed to stop, my father fell
in love with another woman and my parents ended up
getting divorced. I was seven at the time. My oldest
brother went to live with my father, and my younger
brother and I stayed with my mother.

Because of her drug habit, my mother had hardly any
social contact, and now that my father was gone she lived
a very lonely life. At first, as a reaction to the divorce, she
turned to alcohol. This was a terrible period because the
alcohol made her quite aggressive, and of course we suffered as a result. Later she went back to drugs again and
also involved me and my brother. She took cocaine and
she gave us some as well. I was seven years old when I
had my first experience with drugs. I sniffed cocaine and
I still clearly remember what happened the first time. I felt
very energetic and immediately started tidying up the

whole house. From that time my mother fairly regularly gave me coke. My brother stopped when my mother no longer gave us any; from then on he only really smoked hash but, apart from a few short periods, I never really stopped using it. When she didn't give me any more, I made sure that I got my own.

From the time that my father left, my relationship with my mother also changed a great deal. I was the oldest child left at home, and in retrospect I think she saw me as a sort of substitute boyfriend. She told me about her worries and problems and I started to feel very responsible for her. I was a very sensitive child anyway, and was always inclined to put others before myself. She also made me feel terribly guilty; I always felt guilty about her life — as if there were anything I could do about it.

This never really got any better, even when she had a new boyfriend. I didn't get on with him at all. He was English and constantly humiliated me. He said I wasn't worth anything and couldn't do anything, so I started to feel very inferior.

He was also a drug dealer, not only in Holland, but internationally. I hated him, but I must admit that he made sure I could read, and looking back I'm grateful to him for that. Because we were illegal we hadn't had any education. My brother and I usually played in the street and we were never bored there. My mother didn't think it was necessary to go to school, but when I was ten my stepfather decided that I did have to go to school. It wasn't for long because we started travelling soon afterwards, but I was in the fourth year of the primary school for six months and that was all the education I've had in my life.

When we went to live in Portugal later on, he gave me books, and at least I had had an educational basis and could teach myself to read with what I had learnt at school. I loved reading and now I am very glad that I am able to.

Apart from that, the man was a scoundrel. He forced my mother to help him with his drug dealing. She was lonely and crazy about him and therefore she was an easy victim. We travelled with him to India several times to fetch hash which would be smuggled in her luggage. If we'd been caught, she would've carried the can. That's really mean. If it had made her rich it might not have been so bad, but she was only given 25 guilders a day for food, and no more. She never got the money he said he'd put into a bank account for her.

After a while she met a Dutch man and married him. This finished after a year and we left to go back to Liverpool. I was eleven years old by this time. My mother's mother still lived in England, and my mother just wanted to go back to her own country and her own family to try and finish with drugs and alcohol again. At first, she actually succeeded with her mother's help, but when she heard after about seven months that my father had hanged himself, we left to go back to Holland because all sorts of things had to be arranged, and everything started all over again.

I thought it was terrible that my father was dead. Although I hadn't seen him very often, I loved him very much. He was a soft-hearted, sensitive man and treated me like a friend. For example, I remember having a shower with him. He taught me how a man should wash himself. This is a very important memory to me. I think he committed suicide from a feeling of guilt, because he'd sent some people to get drugs from Peru and they'd been caught and put in prison. Knowing my father, I think that he felt terrible about this, and in the end he couldn't cope with it.

My brother, who was living with my father, found him. He couldn't sleep and wanted to go and get his book from the living room when he saw my father hanging there. It must have been terrible for him. He went to live with my father's friends who fostered him.

I never really expressed my sadness about his death. I had had so many experiences that I had repressed all my feelings. With so much misery, you stop caring. It was only six weeks ago, when I went to his grave, that I felt anger and sadness, and I really battered the ground in my fury.

When we returned to Holland my mother got back together with my stepfather. The man she had officially married had completely disappeared. My stepfather had kept in contact with her because he could use her for his trade. So we left for Spain to go and get a quantity of hash which had been smuggled from Morocco. We lived in a camper on the beach on the Costa del Sol.

In retrospect, it seemed that the whole operation took a year and a half altogether. The hash had to be brought from Morocco to Spain on surfboards, and therefore we were very dependent on the weather. It had to be done at night, there couldn't be any moonlight, and the sea had to be absolutely calm.

The venture was only successful after a year and a half. Not that this was a problem for me, because my brother and I had a wonderful time. It was just like paradise, beautiful countryside, the sun always shone and we could spend all day surfing and roller-skating. This was the best part of my life. While other children of my age were sitting at school doing sums, I was learning about life through practical experience. For example, you don't get to know about people from books. You learn about people by doing things with them, and I had ample opportunity for that. Obviously not all my experiences were positive experiences, but I did learn a great deal, especially from travelling, and I'm really glad that I experienced that side of life.

My brother and I were always together. We had a very strong relationship, though this suffered later when I was about fourteen, because of the drugs I was using. Fortunately, our relationship has mended now.

After Spain, we went back to Holland, and from there to Portugal and France for a time. Later on, we only travelled to and fro without staying for months. We also went to Sweden and India.

When I was thirteen, my mother, my brother and I left for India to go and live there. As we had already been there four times, my mother thought it would be wonderful to stay.

My stepfather had told my mother that he had put 100,000 guilders in a bank account for her. This is what she was supposed to have earned on her previous trips. He said he would transfer this money in instalments once we lived there, but once we were there we didn't hear from him again. We had no money to eat and therefore none to get back to Holland. Whether we wanted to or not we had to stay there.

We went to live in a small village; at first in a beautiful house, but when it became clear that no money was coming we soon had to move to something simpler.

In the end we lived there for a year and a half, the last nine months in a sort of pigsty. Fortunately we were able to get work for a while. My brother worked for a baker and I worked in the paddy fields, where I planted and harvested the rice. I worked from seven o'clock in the morning to seven o'clock in the evening for fifty pence a day. That's nothing of course, but it's just enough to live on for a day. Later on, when we didn't have any work, we were kept alive by an Indian woman who sold fruit. She had her own family and several children and gave us food as well. This really impressed me. She had virtually nothing herself, and in the end she had to borrow money to live. It's because of what these people did for us that I have so much respect for poor people. They had nothing, but they would do anything for each other. I learned a great deal from them. Actually, I would have liked to stay there. You didn't have anything, but in a way you had everything — at least, that's how it felt.

Later when we were back home we sent her fifteen hundred dollars to thank her. We felt we had to do that. If she hadn't been there, we would really have died of starvation.

It was in India that I became addicted to heroin. My mother had been using it for a long time and I usually went to get it for her from the Afghani people who lived there. Once I had some myself, and of course that was it. Before that time I'd only taken coke or hash.

It was a miracle how we eventually managed to get back to Holland. One day, an acquaintance of my mother whom she hadn't seen for fifteen years turned up in that small village in India. He just fell out of the sky. It was simply incredible. I'm convinced that he was sent by God, he must have been. He gave us money for the trip to Bombay and to stay in a hotel for a few days so that we could arrange our trip home. That cost £200. We still had the return tickets to fly back to Amsterdam. Of course, my mother did have to do something in return. This man was another hash dealer, and she had to smuggle two bottles of hash oil in her luggage. That was the price for her help.

Shortly afterwards, my stepfather was caught with drugs on the border with France and was sentenced to prison for seven years. It was what he deserved. We haven't heard a thing from him since.

When we got back to Amsterdam, we found that the house where we'd been living before we left had been pulled down. Only a heap of rubble was left. This was

really terrible for us, because we were still illegal, and
that meant that we simply couldn't find anywhere to live.
We ended up in a hostel for the homeless, which wasn't
much fun, but on the other hand, the organization helped
us to get a legal status. It turned out that my mother had
not been officially divorced from her Dutch husband and
therefore the matter was soon settled.

When I was sixteen, I fell in love with a boy for the first
time, and I had a relationship with him. He turned out to
be involved in prostitution, so I soon got to know that
world and I became active myself as well. I found it easy
to earn a great deal of money and men paid me a lot of
attention. I really enjoyed that because I had never had
any attention before. That's really why I started with it. Of
course, the money was good as well, but that wasn't the
main thing. Really it was the attention. I just didn't want
to know that these men weren't really interested in me
but only in sex. I only realized that it was all a con later
on.

I earned enough money to live in hotels, to eat well and
to buy beautiful clothes and drugs. I thought that was
great.

I soon broke off with the first friend when I met an
older man and I fell head over heels in love with him. I
was seventeen when I had a relationship with him.

I didn't know — though he did — that he had AIDS.

He didn't take any precautions to avoid infecting
others and I was too much in love to think about it. As a
prostitute I always practised safe sex, but with him I
didn't think about it. Once, when I asked him about a
painting in his house and he told me it was from a friend
who had died of AIDS, it didn't take me long to realize
that he might have it as well. In fact, he later died of
AIDS, so I'm sure that it was he who infected me. I was
an addict but I had never injected heroin at that time, so

I couldn't have got it from a needle. I was regularly given methadone by the clinic of the municipal health service because I was an addict, and at a certain point I had the opportunity to have a test, so I did. I wasn't really surprised when they told me I was HIV positive; I knew it really. This was at the end of 1986, when I was eighteen years old.

After my first panic reaction I was rather glad. I thought that at least I would die now and would not have to suffer everything that my mother had suffered. I was glad to be saved all that misery. But in fact I had no idea at that time, what it meant to die. I thought that you simply died and that was that, but it's not that simple. By now, I've realized that. It's a process of disintegration and that's terrible.

After a bit, I simply ignored the thought of dying, but when I became ill with serious pneumonia in 1990, when I was twenty-two, I was diagnosed as having AIDS, and that changed everything. I realized that I really would die soon and for the first time in my life I cried my heart out. In itself, this was quite a new experience for me.

Shortly after my AIDS diagnosis, I went to live on my own. I was able to rent a council house and the AIDS foundation gave me some money to furnish it. I was over the moon but as I kept getting ill I turned back to drugs. I just couldn't bear the thought of dying. After a while I went back to live with my mother and things were really bad there.

For the last six months, I've been living in a nursing home. I was too weak to look after myself and I'd neglected myself terribly. When I was at my mother's, I was only interested in drugs. I no longer ate, and my brother saw me getting weaker and weaker. He alerted the hospital department which takes care of patients with AIDS who use drugs. Eventually it was decided to admit me to this nursing home and I gave notice to stop renting the house where I'd been living. I'll stay here now. At first this was terribly difficult. In my life, I'd never lived in one place and obeyed the rules, and it was quite a struggle for me to accept it. I also found it very difficult to accept advice from other people. I had always decided for myself whether I could do something or not; whether something was good or bad. Here there are rules which I must follow; that's how it has to be. Now that I've got used to it, I also see the good side. I've started to see the other people who live here and the group leaders more and more as my new family and I really feel good about that.

The fact that there are people who notice that I have problems and pay attention to them is fantastic. I'm not used to it. It gives me the feeling that I exist and that it matters how I feel. These are all new experiences for me and I am really glad about it. I try to do my bit as well. For example, I clean my own room and try to help where I can. This gives me a sense of self-respect.

Meanwhile, I've also got a boyfriend and that's really fantastic. Although we are both in the same boat and he has AIDS as well, we try to enjoy everything that there still is to enjoy, and we support each other whenever necessary. He's older than I am; I've noticed that I always fall in love with older men. With him I feel safe and protected. I think this is probably because I didn't have a father. But apart from that, our relationship is quite equal.

Sometimes I'm surprised that I'm not angry with the man who infected me. The only answer I have is that I was in love with him. That's why I can't be angry with him. He didn't really love me; that's quite clear from the fact that he brought death upon me. If you do that sort of thing, there can't really be any love. That's clear to me and it hurts.

My life has been totally changed by AIDS. It has become very rich. I feel as though I've started a completely new life. Because I was admitted to the nursing home, I was taken out of the world of drugs and this saved my life. If I'd stayed at home, I would have been dead by now, I'm sure of that. Because of being here I have been able to distance myself from the life I was leading. This changes everything. When you take drugs, nothing else interests you, everything revolves around drugs. Everything, even food, because when you spend too much money on food, you don't have any to buy drugs. What a life it was. Thank God it's over.

At last I have a feeling that I'm alive and I can do and enjoy things which are fun. For example, going to the countryside. I enjoy this so much now. I never used to notice the flowers and the birds singing, but now I go to the park to look and listen, and it's wonderful.

Because of the drugs I had completely lost touch with my feelings. I didn't feel anything, everything passed me by, but luckily this is all over now and I feel so rich. I can feel more, see more and experience more than I've ever done. I have friends around me and I live with people where I feel I belong. Every day I feel happy when I get up, happy to be alive and to enjoy myself.

I have consciously said goodbye to my mother. We were always very dependent on each other. Since I was small I have felt very responsible for her. This was partly because she always made it clear that she found life very difficult. The pressure this put on me was enormous. That's why I was never really able to separate myself from her. Even when I wasn't living with her, I worried about her.

Now she is forty-eight years old and still addicted. I think this is terrible. When you are addicted, your

only concern is to get the drugs you want. It takes over
your whole life so there is no time for social contact or
anything else, and therefore no time for me. Of course
this hurts a lot because I don't have much time left.
I understand now that the tie I thought I had with her
was only an illusion. The tie only existed as a grati-
fication from the drugs. I have been living in this nursing home for six months now and she hasn't visited me
once.

Although this is all very difficult and sad, I also feel a
sense of liberation because of the distance which I can
now feel between her and me. Increasingly I can accept
that she will never be as I would have liked her to be, and
this is already a big step forward for me.

I'd love her to stop using drugs. Then we could use the
time while I'm still alive to really discover each other and
do nice things together like enjoying going to the park.
That would be a consolation to her when I am dead. But
she has to want to do it herself, I can't do it for her. I
must let her go, no matter how hard it is for me. I'm going
to die and I must invest the energy I still have in myself,
otherwise that will be the end of me, and I don't want
that. But I continue to hope that she will change before I
die; for her sake as well as mine. The way things are is so
hopeless.

I visit her from time to time, together with my cousin.
I find it difficult to go on my own. We have always influenced each other a great deal: either she would turn back
to drugs after a period of being clean because I was using
them, or vice versa. I don't want this to happen again. I
feel so impotent when I see her going downhill. I love her
very much and I understand why she got hooked on
drugs after such a terrible childhood. Basically my mother
is a good and very loving person, but she was unable to
cope with life and that's why things have gone as they
have. She even mainlines now and everyone takes advant-

age of her. She lets anyone in because she's so lonely and therefore she's an easy target.

At the moment it's not difficult for me to do without drugs. I am given methadone and I'm trying to stop using that too. Every week I take one pill less. Now I'm on six pills, though I used to take eight. I hope I manage to stop taking them altogether and that my body can take it. It can be very painful because your body can no longer manage without, but I really hope that I succeed.

I don't want to die like I was born — a junkie. Other people succeed in getting qualifications at school; I want to succeed in this. I want to achieve something in life and that's very important to me.

Although I don't have much energy, I feel well at the moment. I've had several problems. I've had pneumonia five times and I'm already blind in one eye.

I'm afraid of dying, very much afraid. Not of being dead, but of dying. I really fear the suffering and the physical deterioration. In this respect, living in a nursing home really confronts you with all this. I see people becoming totally dependent and I find that horrific. The thought that you have to ask for everything is very oppressive. Since I've been living here two people have died and that really frightened me. It brought it all very close. Since the death of these two people I have often thought about my funeral. Before that time I didn't care about it, but now I do. Now I have certain wishes and requirements. The problem is that I'm not insured and so I can't pay for it. I get forty guilders a week and that doesn't leave much. That's why I will be buried by the council and I really mind about that, it makes me feel like a pauper. But I don't know how else it could be done.

I don't believe that life ends after death. I imagine that I will go into the light when I'm dead, and that life there will be better than on earth. My life up to now has been so terribly difficult that, as far as that's concerned, I'm glad I won't live to be eighty. I think things will certainly get better after death. I also believe in reincarnation. I think that in the next life I'll be able to go my own way and really make my own choices. I didn't manage that in this life, but allowed myself to be carried along. However, I'm sure that won't happen to me again. I think it's weak to blame my mother for this; I don't hold it against her, but after all, I was only a child. The fact that I have AIDS is my own fault. I knew that it existed but I still made love without protection. So I can accept that I'm responsible for it myself.

Of course, this was not always the case. I have gone through many stages. I was angry about why this should happen to me and full of despair. For example, about a year ago I cut my wrists in a frenzy of despair. I had just been in hospital and came home with drugs around as usual. I simply couldn't cope with it at all at that moment, and when I woke up one morning I took a piece of glass and started cutting my wrists. Fortunately I didn't cut into a main artery. I'm grateful for that now. I also started drinking heavily for a while, but now I have the feeling that I can really accept it.

I also accept that my life has been as it has. Many people only see the dark side of it, but I wouldn't want to swop with anyone else. There was also another side; I've had many experiences which made me happy and the freedom which I had also had a good side. I am twenty-four years old but I feel much older inside because of everything I've gone through. I don't feel bitter. Sometimes I see bitterness around me and I think that's terrible. It means that you're dead even before you've died.

I hope I live to be old. Twenty-eight seems like quite a good age and I'm twenty-four now. I don't want to be unrealistic: I know that I will die, but if you have no hope it will be over even sooner.

In any case, I'm grateful that I have AIDS. I don't know how long or how short it will take, but at least I have experienced something of life because of this illness.

June 1992

On December 13, 1992, Paul died after an epileptic fit. He was in his twenty-fifth year.

He started with great courage to reduce the dose of methadone, but found it impossible to keep this up. His body could not manage without. Twice he was caught taking drugs. He suffered greatly from feeling that the dope was stronger than he was.

His contact with his mother remained much the same as it had been: as good as nothing. Twice she went to a drug rehabilitation centre but both times unsuccessfully. During his last hours in intensive care, she was with him. Although he was in a coma, he clearly responded to her presence.

Through a collection organized by his friends, Paul was able to realize some of his wishes for his funeral. So he worked very consciously for the preparation of his funeral, even designing his coffin with the help of a cabinet-maker. It was also possible for him to be buried close to his father.

On the gravestone made for him was written the text which he had asked for:

Life goes on.

December 1992

Supporting Organizations

The Metgezel Foundation

The Metgezel Foundation is an independent organization which provides the special kind of help offered by Buddies. It has been operating in Amsterdam since July 1990 for people with AIDS, irrespective of their sex, sexual preference or philosophy. In Holland, Metgezel is the first organization to make use of spiritual ideas — particularly anthroposophical ideas — about illness, death and life, to provide spiritual support for the Buddies in their constant encounter with illness and death.

Metgezel does not impose its own philosophy on anyone, and no one is turned away. In the past two years it has looked after thirty-seven people: twenty-three men and fourteen women (including one child). Eighteen of these have died.

Twenty Buddies have volunteered for this work. They help AIDS patients to think about their problems and arrange practical matters, accompany them to doctors and other appointments, or sometimes to a film or a concert. But they are also there to think about the questions of life, illness and death or simply as company. Their help is free.

Metgezel does not receive any government subsidies and is therefore completely dependent on covenants and gifts from people who support this work.

For information you can write to: Stichting Metgezel, Ita Wegmanhuis, Weteringschans 74, 1017 XR Amsterdam, Netherlands.

Organizations in the United Kingdom

Terrence Higgins Trust
52-54 Grays Inn Road
London WC1X 8JU
071-242 1010
Telephone and face-to-face counselling on every issue from testing to coping with positive diagnosis. Also support for partners and families to help them carry on living.

National AIDS Trust (NAT)
14th Floor, Euston Tower
286 Euston Road
London NW1 3DN
071-383 4246
NAT aims to focus a united response to AIDS from all sections of society, principally by promoting and coordinating voluntary initiatives.

Haemophilia Society
123 Westminster Bridge
London SE1 7HR
071-928 2020
There are thirty local groups around the country offering self-help and support to people affected by haemophilia.

Steps in Time
141 Newham Way
London E16
071-473 5867
A self-advocacy group for young people under the age of 26 living with HIV/AIDS.

Positive Youth
51b Philbeach Gardens
London SW9 9EB
071-373 7547
Positive Youth offers information, advice, support and counselling to young people (under 26) affected by HIV/ AIDS.

Catholic AIDS Link
PO Box 646
London E9 6QP
071-485 7298
A Catholic group offering non-judgmental spiritual, emotional, practical and financial support to those affected by HIV and AIDS.

Agencies and groups (such as Buddies) specializing in helping people with AIDS can be contacted through local hospitals.